THE EVERYTHING SELLING BOOK

How to be a successful salesperson even if you've never sold before

Marguerite Smolen

Adams Media Corporation
Holbrook, Massachusetts

An Everything Series Book.
"Everything" is a trademark of Adams Media Corporation.

Published by
Adams Media Corporation
260 Center Street, Holbrook, MA 02343. U.S.A.

ISBN: 1-58062-319-0

Printed in the United States of America.

J I H G F E D C B A

Library of Congress Cataloging-in-Publication Data
Smolen, Marguerite.
The everything selling book / by Marguerite Smolen.
p.   cm.
Includes index.
ISBN 1-58062-319-0
1. Selling. I. Title.
HF5438.25 .S643   2000
658.85--dc21   99-055543

Interior illustrations by Barry Littmann and Eulala Connor/Portfolio Solutions.

This book is available at quantity discounts for bulk purchases.
For information, call 1-800-872-5627.

Visit our home page at http://www.adamsmedia.com

Dedication

For my father, Francis E. Smolen, once a salesman
and forever a wonderful human being.

Contents

CONTENTS

CONTENTS

Introduction: Anyone Can Sell

If you've picked up this book, you already know that generating sales is a critical—perhaps even the most important—aspect of business. A company without a professional sales effort simply cannot stay in business!

This is true whether you are working for yourself, working for someone else, working out of your home, or working in a major corporation. Sales generate the business that keeps *you* in business.

But if you have little or no sales experience, the art of selling may appear somewhat mysterious. After all, haven't you heard a million times that "salespeople are born, not made"? Well, don't you believe that! Talk to any sales trainer or manager and they'll tell you that many people who think they have a God-given talent for sales turn in mediocre performances, while others who have never viewed themselves as salespeople end up with brilliant track records.

And here's a surprising fact. *If you are a beginner at sales, you have a better chance to succeed than if you've been in sales for years!* How can that be true? you ask.

The Advantages of Being a Beginner

Many seasoned salespeople fall into the trap of believing they "know it all." Over the years, they've honed their methods until they perform them by rote. They've given their favorite sales pitches so many times, their voice sounds like a broken record—even to themselves. They start to become lazy or overconfident. They drop the techniques that helped them achieve their initial success in sales and that hooked them on selling in the first place. Eventually, they may even become inflexible in their approach, resistant to trying new methods, and resentful of management. "Oh, that will never work," they say when someone presents them with a new idea. "I don't have time for that."

The problem here is not technique—it's attitude! It's taking success for granted while overlooking the work that needs to be done to make success happen. Seasoned sales reps forget: *Even a sales method that looked stale yesterday can become a fresh, exciting approach when applied by a person who has a new and different mindset—a beginner's mindset!*

The Truth Is, Anyone Can Learn to Sell

Great salespeople are not born—they are individuals who have worked hard to acquire skills, just as in any other profession.

Cultivating a Beginner's Mindset

If having lots of experience is the key to success, it would not be so difficult to "teach an old dog new tricks." Ask yourself, Why is it so easy for children to learn something new? Why is my three-year-old nephew more confident using the computer than some of my fifty-year-old friends? The three-year-old is not experienced enough to be caught up in limiting beliefs about what he can or cannot do!

So, if you know nothing about sales, and you *know* you know nothing, you are indeed fortunate. This book will provide you with a wealth of information about one of the most exciting, creative, and challenging aspects of being in business—selling. To start with, those who need to gain a sense of control over their sales effort will appreciate the book's structured approach to selling. The simple step-by-step methods presented in the following chapters are highlighted with tips and check boxes that are easy reminders of essential points made in the text. Sample record sheets, worksheets, correspondence, and other paperwork useful to any basic sales effort are contained in the appendices.

But this book offers you something more than a bread-and-butter approach to selling. You also get an abundance of techniques and exercises that you can experiment with to enhance your sales effort in less obvious ways. *This book offers a wholistic approach to selling!* Nothing is more important to a sales effort than the motivation and mindset of the salesperson. With this goal in mind, you'll find the text peppered with motivational exercises designed to help you achieve mastery over your inner salesperson. Remember: The person who is going to make your sales effort the great success it has the potential to be is YOU.

Let's get started!

CULTIVATING A BEGINNER'S MINDSET

In the Far East, for more than one thousand years, a way of living and thinking has persisted among successful individuals that has enabled them to achieve seemingly incredible mental, spiritual, and physical heights. Recently, this behavioral system has had a profound influence in the West as many elite athletes, successful business leaders, and stress-reduction experts claim that their achievements are the result of following the *tao*, or "the way," as the word for this system of philosophy translates.

One of the key practices of Taoism is cultivating a "beginner's mind." In simplest terms, this means that you should approach the task you set for yourself with an empty mind. Too often, when we set goals for ourselves and fail to meet them, it is because our minds are too full to absorb the information needed to achieve the goal. The mind can be filled with all sorts of things—negative beliefs, outmoded ways of doing things, distracting thoughts and influences—that prevent us from focusing on the present, the task at hand. Cultivating a beginner's mind, on the other hand, opens us up to possibility and assists in removing self-limiting beliefs.

You can prepare the way for success in sales by cultivating a beginner's mindset. Practice the following principles of Taoism:

- *Know nothing.* Empty your mind of all preconceived notions about selling and tell yourself, "I know nothing about sales…I'm here to learn." Mean it!

- *Engage in a willing suspension of disbelief.* When you find yourself thinking, "It would be impossible to…" tell yourself, "Let's act as if it were possible to…"

- *Stay focused in the present.* Cultivate total absorption in the activity that faces you now, whether it's dialing the phone or making a presentation. Don't obsess or ruminate about yesterday or tomorrow. If guilt about something you did yesterday or fears for the future enter your mind, let them go and concentrate single-mindedly on the present.

- *Question authority (as the bumper sticker says).* When you find yourself acting judgmental about a buyer's personality or beliefs, or about your own abilities, STOP! Ask yourself, "What if just the opposite is true?" Ask yourself if this belief or judgment puts limitations on your behavior. If it does, don't buy into it!

CHAPTER 1

What You Can Learn from This Book

E ach year, many books are published that claim to offer readers "a new, unique approach to selling." Often these books start by panning traditional sales techniques. They promise the reader great results if only he or she follows the author's exclusive new selling strategy.

This isn't one of those books. I don't want to sound jaded, but in my years of attending sales seminars and training sessions and making sales calls, I've discovered there's some truth to the old adage, There's nothing new under the sun. Traditional, time-proven sales techniques are used by most salespeople—because they work!

In *The Everything Selling Book*, you won't learn just one sales technique, you'll learn dozens! When you go on a sales call, you won't have just one approach at your disposal, you'll have every major sales technique in your repertoire.

Checklist for a Successful Sales Campaign

We'll start by showing you how to manage a sales campaign from start to finish. We'll begin with very basic strategies, such as the following:

- Assembling the tools you need to sell
- Creating a system for selling
- Organizing your sales efforts
- Getting leads
- Rating your prospects
- Meeting and greeting clients
- Identifying decisionmakers
- Making a basic sales call
- Making a presentation
- Overcoming objections
- Closing a sale
- Following up
- Servicing the client

Sales Techniques

After helping you plan a successful sales campaign, we'll take a look at the sales approaches that professionals find most helpful to use. You'll learn how to decide when to use which approach. You'll learn how to figure out what your client's needs are, and which sales approach is likely to interest your prospect. We'll show you why a certain sales approach works—and when you're better off using another one. We'll show you the pluses and minuses of:

- Product-focused selling
- The benefits sell
- Selling against the competition
- Selling on price
- Selling by categories
- The "soft sell"
- Numbers-focused selling
- The problem-solution sell
- Consultive selling
- The added-value sale

and more!

Personal Skills You'll Need to Develop

And because the way a salesperson approaches the selling process can make or break a sale, *The Everything Selling Book* is more than just a sales "primer." We'll also tackle some of the more challenging issues faced by the sales professional. We'll help you build your people skills, so by the time you are finished with this book, you'll be able to:

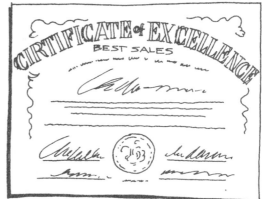

- Break the ice
- Figure out what your prospect's true issues are
- Discover what the decision-making process is for your client
- Establish rapport and trust
- Control a sales call
- Build interest in your product or service
- Handle conflict and deal with tough questions
- Negotiate terms
- Defend yourself when necessary
- Overcome common selling obstacles
- Avoid common sales mistakes

and, most important of all:

- Partner with your client to create a win-win situation

Having a positive outlook is important for succeeding at life in general, and sales in particular. Many people are wary of entering the profession because they have a preconceived notion that "salespeople are born, not made." They are afraid they don't have the "sales gene." What they mean is that they fear they don't have the right personality to succeed at sales. In fact, anyone can be successful at sales if they follow the tried-and-true steps outlined here. But it's easy to become discouraged if you aren't successful 100 percent of the time—and, let's face it, no one is ever 100 percent successful! Because the motivation and mindset of a salesperson are all-important, especially when things don't go perfectly, in *The Everything Selling Book* we'll also teach you ways to:

- Stay motivated in your sales effort
- Deal with rejection
- Protect yourself from sales burnout
- Build morale and self-esteem
- Garner respect from others
- Network for success
- Focus on your goals
- Maintain enthusiasm and enjoy your job
- Become a successful sales professional

Selling is an easy-to-learn profession. All most people need is a little guidance, which *The Everything Selling Book* is happy to provide. If you're unsure of your ability to succeed at sales, don't sweat it! Sales is a challenging profession, but a highly rewarding one for those who succeed. It's only natural for you to feel insecure at the start of a new profession, but rest assured, the rewards are worth the risk.

In choosing to read this book, you're off to a great start in a rewarding new career!

Using this book is super-easy! Graphic pointers highlight the most important pieces of information and ideas. Here's what the icons mean:

Key Ideas. We know you don't always have time to read everything in detail. Look for this icon when you need a quick "refresher" on key points or creative sales ideas.

Attitude Adjustment. It's not what you know, it's not even who you know. It's how you use what you know that creates success! To "psych" yourself up, maintain professionalism, and shape a positive outlook about selling, check out the explanations and exercises marked with this icon.

Checklist. Do you need help focusing? Our checklists outline key tasks, making it easy for you to take the next step—or series of steps.

Dialogue Boxes. Practice talking to clients by reviewing these sample sales dialogues.

Your Mission, Should You Accept It...

Know Why
You're Doing What
You're Doing

To be successful at anything, it helps to know who you are and where you are going.

Selling Is a Perspective on Life

Because few people are encouraged to think of selling as a profession, many people fall into it by accident. They turn to selling when few other job possibilities exist. They turn to selling because they think it's a way to make a lot of money without needing a special degree, a particular talent, or job experience. They turn to selling in order to become involved in a field they love but are unable to economically participate in—as is the case when a designer who can't earn a living making and selling his or her own creations takes a job behind the counter in a jewelry store.

Selling is all of these things—and so much more. *Selling is a perspective on life.* When you think about selling as a second-best option, you are limiting your world view and your own possibilities. You are limiting how high you can go in life.

Now, I know that sounds a bit overblown, but believe me: No amount of knowledge or technique will help you achieve your goal, whether it's in the world of sales or elsewhere, unless you feel that what you're doing has meaning and purpose. Without purposefulness, you won't follow through on what you know you're supposed to be doing. You'll lose concentration and undermine yourself. You'll find a thousand and one excuses not to do what needs to be done. *You'll be so depressed when you hear the word* no *from a prospect, your whole world will fall apart!*

So at the very beginning, when you first start out in sales, you need to get all of your skeletons out of the closet and start addressing them one by one. You need to figure out why you're selling. Why are you reading this book? Do you think of yourself as a salesperson? Why or why not?

Selling is a process of setting goals and achieving them. This sounds pretty simple; but along the path to accomplishing a goal, there can be many challenges. Because salespeople are so success oriented, they often obsess

about failure. They speak of sales as a battlefield where winning is the only option.

No wonder so many people burn out in sales! When you view your daily life as a battlefield where rejection is not an option if you are to be successful, you are setting yourself up for burnout. In sales, you will always come across more noes than yeses. No wonder salespeople often say that the biggest difficulty they face is rejection and that they had to leave the profession because they found it too demoralizing.

That's why, before you begin your sales career, you need to address the concept of failure up-front. Have you ever made a New Year's resolution and not followed through on it? Have you ever set a goal and not accomplished it? If so, you're not alone. At one time or another, most people fall short of achieving a stated goal. Unfortunately, failing to achieve a personal goal can set some people up for greater loss later on, especially if they find themselves continually failing to meet standards they've set for themselves. They start to think about why they can't accomplish their goals, and begin to think there's something wrong with them. They start to believe their own bad press!

Develop a Mission Statement

Is your intention to reap material rewards? Is it to support your family? Is it to help other people? Developing a clear sense of purpose—a personal mission statement—can help you immensely when you are confronted with the daily ups-and-downs of selling. Only when you feel truly comfortable with why you are a salesperson will you be able to enjoy life as a salesperson.

Successful corporations and nonprofit agencies know the truth of this. That's why they write corporate mission statements, print them up, and distribute them to employees and post them on the walls in public lobbies. Right from the start, I suggest that you design a personal mission statement and tack it to the wall to remind you every day of your purpose!

When drafting a mission statement, it isn't enough to list the dollar figures you hope to sell, the material goods you hope to buy thanks to your sales commission, or the outcomes you hope to

KEY IDEAS

Link Selling to What You Value

When our actions don't reflect our values, it causes internal conflict. Internal conflict sets us up for failure.

Personal Mission Statement Form

My company is _____.

My mission is to impact _____.

I plan to build _____.

My vision is _____.

I will be the best _____.

I will be the most efficient _____.

I offer exceptional _____.

I have committed to _____.

My goal is to facilitate _____.

I will inspire _____

    by _____.

My clients are _____.

I impact my clients in a positive way by _____.

I provide my clients with:

    Resources: _____

    Products: _____

My clients will be able to _____

    through the following services _____.

I benefit _____.

My service is outstanding for the following reasons:

    1. _____

    2. _____

3. _____

4. _____

I should be the first choice among the competition because:

We provide _____.

We support _____.

and serve _____.

I model these principles:

1. _____

2. _____

3. _____

4. _____

and show others how to do the same.

By staying true to my vision, ethics, and philosophy. I _____.

I promise to pursue _____,

so I can stay competitive in the business environment today and to _____,

so that I can lead a lifestyle of _____.

For as long as it takes, I will continue to provide _____

to _____

and everyone who needs what I have to offer in the future.

To this end, I dedicate myself to _____.

Don't Become Prey to Extreme Emotions!

Whether negative or positive, they will prevent you from achieving success in the long run. A good sales person knows how to take the good with the bad and moderate highs and lows. Learn to protect your equilibrium!

accomplish (pay for a daughter's education, etc.). Those things are goals, not a mission statement. They can help inspire you, but a mission statement does much more. A mission statement lays out how what you do for a job impacts your total life's purpose.

A mission statement explores values, and to the degree that it mentions goals, it ties values to goals. If you are not aware of your belief system as you pursue your goals, you are not likely to achieve them. When your goals are in conflict with your underlying belief system, you set yourself up for failure.

For example, suppose you value helping other people, and one of your primary goals in life is to give to other people. If you believe that selling is taking other people's money, robbing them of material possessions, how could you possibly succeed at it? If you believe that in order to help people, you need to suffer some kind of martyrdom, how can you expect to be paid fairly for the helpful service you provide?

Writing a mission statement is a three-step process:

1. Identify an important personal value.
2. Define how that value can manifest itself in the sales process.
3. Link the value to a positive outcome for yourself.

For example:

Value. I value helping other people.
Definition of help. I want to help other people so they can meet their goals.
Link. Fair and reasonable fees for my help enable me to continue to help other people.

Now you are positioned to see the sales effort as a means of helping other people meet their goals. Your personal mission statement might be to use sales as a vehicle for helping other people meet their goals and to get paid fairly so that you can grow your efforts to help more and more people over time.

What do you value? Family time? Recognition? Fame? Personal relationships? Money? Growth? Learning new things? Freedom?

Choose one sentence from the following list that reflects your choice of which word to emphasize:

> To succeed at sales, you must *sell*.
> To succeed at *sales*, you must sell.
> To succeed at sales, you *must* sell.
> To *succeed* at sales, you must sell.
> To succeed at sales, *you* must sell.

Did you underline the word *sell*? Perhaps you're limited by the belief that being a salesperson is all about the physical act of selling—learning techniques and applying them. On the plus side, this could mean that you understand that a salesperson is an action-oriented individual who gets up each day and works a program. On the negative side, it could mean that you think selling is simply "going through the motions." As long as you talk to lots of people, you'll succeed. This is true, to a point. But, eventually, you'll want to improve your rate of return.

Underlining *sales* could mean that you think being a salesperson is all about a mysterious process called sales that you are uncertain you'll ever be able to do. The myth of the "born" salesperson stops people from even trying to learn the techniques they need to succeed at sales, and it perpetuates the worst and least successful selling approaches. Demystify the selling process! Recognize that it can be learned and that if you commit to employing the techniques and methods discussed in this book and others, you can become a very successful salesperson indeed!

Did you underline the word *must*? On the positive side, this suggests a high level of motivation, a need to sell. But be careful. "Must" also suggests desperation. Desperate salespeople believe that the customer is doing them a favor each time they "deign" to buy! As a salesperson, it's not only logical but necessary to appreciate your customers. However, becoming filled with doubt about the worthiness of your profession will not help you or your clients. Salespeople who do not value the products they sell or the service they provide are unlikely to succeed at sales in the long run. But it shouldn't be this way! Think what it would be like if you couldn't buy any of the necessities of life or any of the things that give you pleasure. Salespeople perform a worthwhile service by helping people get what they need and want. Know that fact and act as if it were true—it is!

Did you underline the word *succeed*? This suggests a focus on the end goal: success at your endeavor. You may be the sort of person who keeps an eye on the ball and takes a long view of things. By emphasizing the word *succeed*, are you expressing a high level of motivation to be a winner? Perhaps you are the competitive sort who likes to prove you can do it. It's great to have a winning attitude. But being overly competitive is not altogether good. Be realistic: You cannot sell everybody. A good salesperson knows how to take the good with the bad and moderate highs and lows. Learn to protect your equilibrium!

As you can see, each one of these views of selling has pluses and minuses. But there is still one more word in the sentence to underline that we haven't discussed: To succeed at sales, *you* must sell.

You are the most important part of the selling process. Once you realize how important you are to the sales process, you'll realize that, as a salesperson, the ball is truly in your court.

What If They Say No?

Remember when you first learned to ride a bike? Perhaps you started with a three-wheeler. But rather quickly you decided you wanted to be riding on two wheels. So your dad or mom got you a bicycle with two little training wheels attached to either side of the big back wheel. It was better than the tricycle, but you wanted to be one of the big kids, riding around with no training wheels. It was pretty scary, though, to try to ride a bicycle for the first time. You were afraid of falling and getting hurt on the hard pavement. But once you tried riding, you found that it wasn't as scary as it first appeared! If you fell off your bicycle, you didn't break into a million pieces.

In what way is selling like riding a bicycle?

Exercise. Practice these affirmations:

- *I am doing what it takes to get to the next level.*
- *If I learn some basic techniques and practice them, I'll be comfortable selling in a short time.*
- *Even if everything goes completely wrong on a sales call, I can pick myself up and go on to make a great sales presentation on the next call.*

Structure? Spend some time making a list of your values. Now prioritize them. Some values may conflict with others, so it's important to know what is most important to you. For example, if you value stability and freedom, you may find yourself in internal conflict.

Once you have a clear list of your values, ask yourself how these values tie into your core beliefs. Do you associate these values with certain behaviors? Are any of these behaviors self-defeating? If so, can you envision a way to fulfill your core beliefs without subscribing to self-defeating behaviors? What positive steps can you take to embody these values? (The exercise described in the Attitude Adjustment box on page 13 will help you identify limiting beliefs.)

Most important, how can sales be a vehicle for you to accomplish what you truly value?

Writing Your Personal Mission Statement

To make formulating your thoughts easier, it may be helpful to do the following exercises:

1. Call up some organizations or corporations that you admire and ask them to share with you their mission statements or codes of behavior.
2. Write your own personal mission statement and tack it in a visible spot so you can review it on a daily basis. (Make a copy of the worksheet on page 10 and fill it in.)
3. Don't be afraid to add to or edit your mission statement as time goes by!

Know Your "Stuff" and Believe In It.

You can't sell it if you don't believe in it! Taking this concept even farther, you can't sell it if you don't feel it! To best represent a product or service (with sales results that prove it), you need to have experienced the benefits of that product or service. For example, if you sell life insurance, you had better own life insurance so you can have experienced, firsthand, the benefits of it—peace of mind, protecting your family, planning for retirement, etc. Rather than just talking about the benefits theoretically, you can now speak from your heart when a prospective customer asks your opinion about your product or service. Customers know the difference between a learned sales presentation and a heartfelt one.

Stop Selling and Start Listening.

The best approach to Customer-Focused Selling is asking good questions, then listening intently to the answers. Selling is not about talking well; it's the ability to gather information, consolidate the information, and provide a helpful intervention (your product or service). Customers want to talk! They want to tell you about their "world," about their "unique" problems, about themselves! Even if you've heard it a million times before and you know what they are going to say before they say it . . .

let them talk. Customers buy from you based more on how well you listen than on how well you talk. Stop selling and start listening.

Leave Your Ego at the Door and Learn Flexibility.

Can you remember a time when you got in your own way, just by being you? Most experienced sales reps can. The point is, add a healthy dose of flexibility whenever your personal agenda enters into the situation. Let's say you scheduled a one-hour appointment for a sales presentation on human resources consulting services to the president of a midsize company. You've spent hours preparing a beautiful electronic presentation that you feel does a great job of explaining your capabilities. When you walk into the meeting, you find out that there will be three additional people attending; that you have only twenty minutes, not sixty; and that you are one of six consultants they are interviewing that morning. What do you do? You could rush through your presentation because YOU want to do it the way YOU'VE prepared. Or you could put it aside and probably be better off investing your time in establishing trust, credibility, and in making a deeper business connection to each member of the team. Going with your ego could kill that sale; going with flexibility and good judgment could lead to that sale. Keep an open mind and always address the current circumstances.

CHAPTER 3

Your Sales Tool Kit

KEY IDEAS

The Buyer Needs to Be Educated

We live in a vastly more complex world than the world of the door-to-door salesman of decades past, a world inhabited by media-savvy, visually sophisticated consumers. Today, salespeople must do more than just describe the product. They must educate the buyer about the worth of the product in a friendly, articulate fashion. Likewise, a good sales kit does more than simply describe the product. A good sales package educates prospects and addresses their concerns in an easy-to-understand, enjoyable format. The kit helps customers sell themselves the benefits of a company's product or service!

Selling is a profession that services people. As is the case in other service professions—medicine, plumbing, car repair—tools help the sales professional get the job done efficiently and effectively. It's easy to visualize the tools of other trades—doctors have medical kits, painters have a palette and a box full of paints. But what exactly is the salesperson's "tool kit"? Many people never see a sales kit until they enter the selling profession. In its most basic version, a sales tool kit consists of a sample case or sales literature of some kind.

Remember the famous door-to-door brush salesman of decades past? In an era when many companies relied on door-to-door canvassing, he only needed a great product, a sample case, and a simple printed sheet to convey the benefits of purchasing an item to a client.

Why Have a Sales Tool Kit?

Today, most industry sales kits take their cue from the packages of information developed by magazines to sell their product. Long before salespeople made presentations to clients urging them to spend hard-earned dollars via invisible pulses of energy traveling unseen fiber networks (telecommunications), magazines were selling "space"—an invisible audience of consumers the advertiser couldn't see and most likely would never meet.

How would you feel if someone called you and said, Give me thousands of dollars, and I'll provide you with something you can't see or touch! You'd need some convincing, right?

To handle this situation, magazines developed something known in the industry as a "media kit." Today, millions of companies from small mom-and-pop bakeries to manufacturers of toothbrushes and computers use sales kits based on the media kit concept.

If you're working for a major corporation, you will probably be given a package of information that you can use to educate your client about your product or service. Large companies have entire marketing departments devoted to creating demand for a product and producing the necessary sales literature. Many companies also have merchandising departments that devise "added-value" promotions and premiums—everything from free T-shirts to unique

- *More people today sell services rather than products.* The vacuum salesman could throw a little dirt on the floor and his potential customers could watch his nifty machine suck it up. Today's salesperson can't lug around a fancy copying machine, telecommunications network, or, if she is providing personnel of some kind, all of the people she might represent.

- *The products being sold today are more complicated than in the past.* New technologies have affected the way products operate and what they can do. In our globally connected marketplace, production of these products is not as simple as it was before. Your customers have more reason to worry about getting orders delivered in a timely fashion and whether the item they're purchasing will do what it's supposed to do. After-sale support is critical today. Learning to push a button to run a vacuum was pretty simple; learning to operate a computer is less so. And when the network is down or the electronic gizmo you sold stops working, your client will expect you or someone in your company to troubleshoot the problem and get things going again.

- *New technologies and laws have reduced start-up costs, allowing more competition in the marketplace.* Look at the printing industry, for example. Fifteen years ago, to provide a customer with the means to print a colored picture, you needed a $150,000 piece of equipment. Today, you can do nearly the same thing on a piece of equipment that costs $10,000. Lower start-up costs mean more competition and smaller profit margins.

- *Again, due to advances in technology, customers today expect more from products and services, and more from the people selling them.* Customers expect products to do more for them. They also expect shorter turnaround times, higher levels of efficiency, and more and better service.

- *Our media-hyped society has created a customer base that is increasingly visual.* People want to be entertained! They don't want to think. They want to find out what they need to know quickly and painlessly. And they want to enjoy the process of getting that information. They want to see lots of pictures—pretty ones, or pretty interesting ones. An attractive sales kit will help potential clients visualize what they are buying—even if it's something they can't "see"!

Keep Your Image Consistent

Like everyone else, buyers are bombarded with information these days. You need to create a strong brand identity among potential clients. One way to create identity is by being consistent with a brand's image. In the simplest terms, this means that whenever possible, key design elements should appear on all marketing tools. For example, the company logo, ink color, paper color and texture, slogan, and other essential information included on your business card should be used for your stationery, brochures, and other marketing tools. Consistency of design implies reliability in other areas.

merchandise display units to free vacation giveaways. These programs are designed to help convince prospects to buy the product and to help them, in turn, sell the product to their clients. In the grand scheme of things, it's tempting to just consider the salesperson the messenger, and the product, sales literature, and merchandising promotions "the message." But if you are working for yourself—or if your company does not provide you with a marketing or sales kit (for our purposes, they're one and the same thing)—you'll need to assemble one of your own.

Developing a Marketing Kit

A basic sales kit might include your business card and a colorful folder, with an attractive cover bearing the company logo and featuring inside pockets to hold additional sales literature. One of the pockets could have slits to hold your business card. (See Appendix A for a checklist of the elements of a marketing kit.)

Inside the folder, you might put any or all of the following items:

- A letter introducing yourself and summarizing why the prospect would benefit from what you have to sell (See Appendix B for samples of letters of introduction.)
- A printed piece of sales literature that describes the product or service being offered—its history, benefits, and features
- Testimonials from satisfied clients
- Information that is relevant to the industry, especially if it's information that only your company has (e.g., the results of a survey you took)
- Information about your company—what makes it unique, how well it's run, how outstanding its service record is, how it's preparing for change in the marketplace, what its goals are for the future, and how it plans to meet challenges in the years ahead
- Top ten reasons people want to do business with you
- Press clippings—recent magazine or newspaper articles about your company or of interest to people who might want to buy your product

YOUR BUSINESS CARD

One tool that every professional rushes out to get at the start is a business card. The business card includes the company name, address, phone number (with extension, if necessary), fax machine number, and the salesperson's name, title, e-mail address, and cell phone, if available.

Business cards are so common, it's easy to overlook how helpful this basic item can be in starting the sales process. A good business card contains more than just basic information. By paying attention to a few key elements, you can tell a potential customer a lot about what you do and encourage the person to keep it handy or, conversely, to toss it out.

The business card is the first business tool your prospect is likely to see. So you want to make sure that it reinforces what you are selling. Consider including the following elements on your business card:

❑ *The company logo.* The logo should be present on all sales materials, from stationery to brochures. A logo helps establish your company's identity. If your company does not have a logo, you can include a design element that mimics a logo, such as a floral vine if you sell flowers or a pipe wrench if you sell tools for plumbers.

❑ *A slogan or other brief, informative statement that lets the prospect know what you can offer them—in a nutshell.* Perhaps you are a "tech lord" or you are the "hot dog king" or you work for a company that "services travelers worldwide" or you sell "one-of-a-kind historic costumes." If there is room on your card, try to include a line about what it is that you do or have to offer.

❑ *Your title.* It says a lot about what you do. Salesperson, Account Executive, Service Representative all mean the same thing. Which sounds better?

❑ *A typeface that relates to your audience.* If you're selling sneakers, you'll want the typeface to keep your card sporty and fun. If you're selling lingerie, you'll want something more alluring and feminine.

❑ *An ink color and paper that reflect what your business is about.* If you are selling accounting services, a conservative look instills confidence in your prospect. If you are selling a creative service, such as interior design, you'll want something more fashionable. If your company promotes environmentalism, be sure to use recycled paper and investigate printing with soy ink!

Consider Visual Reminders for Restocking

To keep tabs on what needs restocking, tape a copy of the item to the bottom of its bin so if it is ever empty, you'll remember which piece the bin once contained or, to put it another way, which piece you're missing.

- A value-added item, such as a newsletter containing helpful tips for your clients (see Appendix C)
- Press releases about new products or services
- Brief profiles of key players in your company
- A key chain, mug, hat, magnet, tote bag, or other merchandising "gift" bearing your logo
- Problem/solution questions and answers
- Information about the market you service, including geography, if relevant
- Independent statistics that verify your ability to service a market or the quality of your product or how you compare to the competition

You may not need to include all of these sales tools in your initial approach to a client. But you may want to include all of them when you make an important presentation or proposal. So you'll definitely want to have all of these elements available to pull out at a moment's notice.

Depending on your industry, clients, and the cost of the item you're selling, you can add other kinds of media to your sales package. Videos, Web sites, CDs, tape cassettes, and computer disk demos are additional sales tools that you can look into. If you're selling music, then a demo cassette of your band is a must; if you're a beauty salon or cosmetics manufacturer, a video of before-and-after makeovers can be very convincing. But media other than printed materials can be costly and require special equipment to run—and your client will have to set aside precious time to view it.

Later, we'll talk about when and how to use these sales tools, and why it is best to present them to the client in person. But for now, you need to figure out which of these items best tells your company's story. Then establish a budget that reflects your marketing priorities.

Keeping Sales Tools Accessible

So far in this chapter, we've covered some of the tools used by professionals to run a sales campaign. A lot of those tools involved sheets of paper—and we're not through yet. Before we finish, we'll be asking you to generate even more pieces of paper.

In future chapters, we'll cover how to get a sense of a potential customer's current situation (this is known as a precall analysis), how to interview prospects and find out what their needs really are, how to write a follow-up letter, and how to draft a proposal. All of these things involve writing information down on paper or keeping a record in another easily accessible form.

So, before we close this chapter—and before we talk about generating more tools for you to keep track of—let's talk about how to organize the elements of your media kit so they are easy to access when you need them.

Organizing Your Sales Tools

Your method of organization ought to meet the following four requirements:

1. Elements of your sales tool kit must be readily accessible when you are selling in your office.
2. They must be readily accessible when you are selling on the road.
3. You must be able to tell at a glance when the stock for any particular element is running low, so that you, or someone in your organization, can order more—before you run out.
4. If anyone commits the mistake of using the last sales piece before new ones are ordered, you must have a way to get a copy of that piece as a stop-gap measure.

The most efficient system I've found for organizing sales tools isn't very creative, but it does meet these requirements. I use those inexpensive plastic stacking bins that you can buy at any office supply store. If you think you'll be storing large quantities of each item, however, you might want to use shelves.

KEY IDEAS

Keep a Backup

Because we all break our own rules, and we just might find ourselves grabbing the last bit of sales literature before new ones have been ordered, keep one copy of each item in a ring binder. Put them in plastic sleeves so they won't be marred by hole punches, and you'll always have something to copy in case of emergency.

KEY IDEAS

Speedy Follow-up Is Essential

A speedy follow-up to any sales meeting is essential! Following up lets buyers know that you are interested in their business and that you are a professional who can be relied on. Here's a tip that can help make following up with a client easy and effortless: Keep a selection of sales literature, some postcards (naturally designed to promote your company, with your company name, logo, address, and phone number), company stationery, envelopes, and stamps in your car. After each meeting, take a few minutes to jot a message to the prospect on the back of a postcard, and drop it in the nearest mailbox. Or, write a note on the piece of sales literature you promised to send, put it in an envelope, and mail it right away (see Appendix B, for some examples). Whatever you mail is likely to reach them the next day or shortly thereafter. You'll win points from the prospect or client for your thoughtfulness and your promptness in following through. And, when you get back to the office, you'll have given yourself some breathing room. Following up the lead won't seem as overwhelming, since you've already accomplished your initial follow-through!

It helps to put the ingredients you use most in adjacent bins. That way you can grab the top five pieces of information, one after another, and place them in your folder without having to hunt up and down every row of bins each time you assemble a package.

If you plan to have less experienced, temporary help assemble standard packets, or you worry about those times when life's stresses make it difficult for you to remember just how you planned to organize a basic kit, you may want to post an illustration nearby showing what goes where. (I used to think this detail was a bit neurotic, until I saw that the new franchised bagel shop in my neighborhood uses an illustration to remind its employees how to "build" its most popular sandwiches, noting where the lettuce goes as opposed to the cheese and the meat.)

Unlike searching for files in a cabinet, you'll only need a quick glance at the bins to tell you which pieces you have plenty of and which are running low.

Selling out of the Trunk of Your Car

If you travel a lot, you'll need copies of sales pieces to take with you on the road. Depending on how many set appointments you have, you'll want to have a few kits assembled and ready to go. For those times when a client requests more than one kit, or you want to leave information with someone you've just met, or you want to customize a presentation, you'll need to have other pieces readily available.

At any office supply company, you can purchase a lightweight plastic crate to hold the pieces of sales literature. Put them in file folders and arrange them in alphabetical order by the most prominent piece of type on the page or however you find it easiest to identify each piece. Placing the

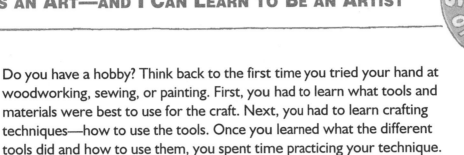

Do you have a hobby? Think back to the first time you tried your hand at woodworking, sewing, or painting. First, you had to learn what tools and materials were best to use for the craft. Next, you had to learn crafting techniques—how to use the tools. Once you learned what the different tools did and how to use them, you spent time practicing your technique. You selected a project to work on and obtained plans or a pattern to follow. Finally, after dedicating yourself to a particular project for a time, you turned out a finished "work of art"!

Learning how to sell isn't much different. You simply need to follow these *eight steps for making a sale.*

1. Assemble the proper tools.
2. Select the best material to work with.
3. Learn how to use the tools.
4. Learn what tools work best on which material.
5. Practice your technique.
6. Set a goal(s).
7. Devote time to your goal(s).
8. Finish what you start.

Exercise: Spend sometime visualizing your favorite hobby, focusing on the enjoyable sensations you felt while you created the project. Then visualize yourself working through the same steps as you sell an imaginary client, associating the same pleasant feelings with the art of selling.

prestuffed folders in the back of the crate will prevent them from getting torn, dirty, and worn while they are stored, however briefly, in your car.

If you need or want something smaller to keep sales literature in, you might try one of those enclosed portable file cases with a handle on the top, accordion-pleated sides, and A–Z tabs inside, or a more contemporary, solid-plastic version of the same without tabs. Any of these storage methods will take up very little space while enabling you to "run your office from your car."

Another reason to carry some of your tool kit with you has to do with follow-up. A key reason many salespeople fail to get a sale after having a successful meeting with a client is that they don't promptly follow up. The client can easily forget who you are, or what you discussed. Once you're back in the office, you can get caught up with tracking down new leads or attending to other work and delay getting back to people as soon as you'd like.

Respect How Your Customer Prefers to Communicate.

You might be fast-paced and outgoing, or maybe you're more reserved and slower-paced. How you like to interact with others should be secondary to how your customer naturally interacts. Be aware of your customer's style of communication and respond accordingly. This is not to say don't be yourself, but rather, honor your customer's preference for style. Remember, nonverbal language is a powerful tool in building a bridge for communication. It's the chemistry side of the sale, the hard-to-put-your-finger-on-it part that says, "I'm not quite sure why but I really like (or don't like) this salesperson." It's your responsibility in selling to be the one who adapts and therefore makes the communication more comfortable and more effective. The end result is that customers who feel that you communicate on their wavelength will open up to you more readily, be more forthcoming with information, and trust you more rapidly.

Plant Triggers and Leave Footprints.

Make it easy for your prospective customers to work with you. Planting triggers means that every time you interact with an existing customer or a prospective customer, you provide them with "triggers," or reasons why they might need to work with you or buy from you. For example, if you are selling advertising specialties and the prospect doesn't seem to be particularly interested in doing business now, provide them with triggers by saying, "Some of the clients we work with use mugs at trade shows, water bottles on the Fourth of July, and hats for the first day of summer." The trigger you're giving the prospect is that of dates and events. You want them to think of you if a date or event triggers a need for your product. Next, make sure you leave "footprints," which are the ways a customer can find you again if they need you. Some of these you probably use now—a business card or a company brochure. But how about a newsletter, written articles, advertising in a local paper, an easy-to-remember 800 number, a memorable company name, sending them a postcard from your office location, or maybe a calendar to hang on their wall all year? The objective of planting triggers and leaving footprints is to make it easy for your customers to remember and find you when thinking of your product or service. Exactly what you want!

Manage Yourself Like a Business.

You know the saying "Time is money." On the money side, businesses focus on both revenue and profitability. In sales, the tendency is toward focusing only on revenue. Look at how you operate, and include the principles of good business with a review of time, money, and profit. Segment your accounts and determine the gems. Look for the ones that are most profitable, the ones that have the most potential, and those that can keep a stream of revenue with the least amount of handholding. You might find that Pareto's Rule of 20/80 is true, that 80 percent of your sales come from 20 percent of your accounts. As any business should, simply ask yourself how you can do more business with those kinds of accounts and manage the other accounts differently. Your time is your money. Invest your time in the places that generate the most profit.

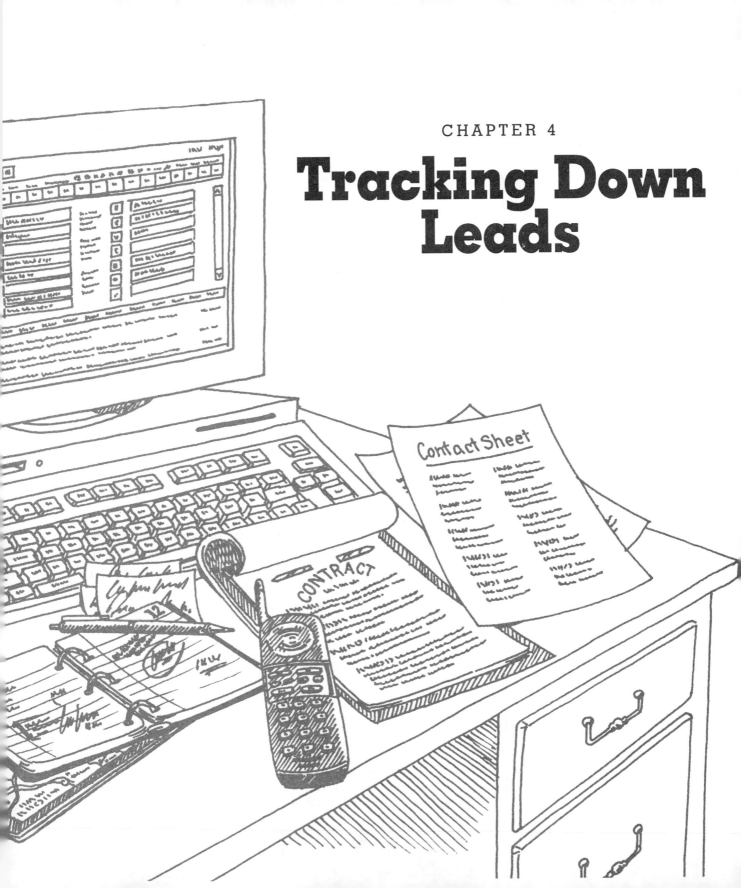

CHAPTER 4

Tracking Down Leads

Although we've talked about prospects, we haven't said much about prospecting itself. Where do you find potential buyers, or "leads" as they're often called? In this chapter, we'll tell you.

Starting at the Top: Your "Best Bets"

There's an adage I've heard so many times in sales seminars, it's worth repeating here: 80 percent of your business comes from the same 20 percent of customers. Now, if, like me, you've always hated math, don't let the percentages throw you. All this sentence means is that in every business, out of the total number of customers you do business with, you'll find that there are a few—about 20 percent—who will be spending the most on whatever you have to sell.

Sometimes this 20 percent will consist of customers you just happen to bond well with, but generally, they'll be clients that everyone in your industry finds worthwhile pursuing. Perhaps these customers are so large and need so many items, they buy from many suppliers. You, too, can count on some dollars from them. Or perhaps they do business with many people because they find it necessary to maintain their position in a particular industry, so anyone who can provide them with an audience is worthy of a few dollars.

Just look around you. What two soft drinks are promoted the most? All over the place, from billboards, to magazine ads, to vending machines, to paper cups . . . even the glasses filled with another beverage in a restaurant may have the Coca-Cola logo on them. If you took the time to scan the shelves in your local supermarket, you'd see that there are many other types and brands of drinks on the shelves. Visit a gourmet or health-food store, and you'll see even more drinks. But with all of the variety that exists, Coke and Pepsi are still the two main beverages seen in ads in just about every major magazine. These companies fall into the 20 percent category for many advertising and marketing executives.

Six Sources for Leads

Source #1: Follow the Competition

Identify the top 20 percent—the top business accounts—in your industry, and go after them. Most likely they'll already be buying from a competitor. In fact, you should try to figure out where your competition is selling, and pursue these accounts. The accounts that are buying from your competitor are already in the market for what you have to sell. They have already been qualified—by the competition! It's often so difficult to locate fresh, qualified prospects that you are much better off going after an account even if you think your competition is solidly entrenched there. You owe it to yourself and your potential clients to let them know what you have to offer, especially if it's something unique. And it always will be unique, because you are part of the deal! Even if you are selling a similar product, the competition won't have you. You can bring fresh, new energy, better service, and so much more to the deal!

Source #2: The Other 80 Percent

Maybe everyone is going after the big guys. Maybe no one is servicing the little guys. Is there an ignored, neglected, or forgotten segment of the industry that needs attention and isn't getting it? For example, many printers specialize in short-runs, printing one hundred to a thousand copies of something at a time. Yet other printers only want to handle press runs of one hundred thousand or more. A few smart printers decided that the guy in the middle—the guy who needed to print between twenty-five thousand and one hundred thousand copies of something—needed attention. So they went after that segment of the market. Often there are businesses that feel neglected because everyone is focusing on the giants in the industry. Yet the little guys, added up, can mean big business. I remember how surprised I was to learn from an advertising director I once worked with that the newspaper's classified ad section brought in many more dollars per page than the pages featuring large, fancy space ads!

KEY IDEAS

A Minority of Customers Provide a Majority of Business

Seasoned sales reps talk about the 80/20 rule. Translation: 80 percent of your business will come from 20 percent of your clients.

Source #3: Pull from Qualified Lists

Many people before you have assembled lists of prospects. Some of these lists are free; others are available for a fee. Here are a few suggestions.

- *The reference section of your library.* You'll find a great selection of books listing businesses that fit a variety of criteria.
- *Your local computer store.* You'll find CD-ROMs for sale that list virtually every business in the country—although they typically list only the SIC (industry) code and perhaps the estimated annual sales or number of employees instead of giving a description.
- *The World Wide Web.* Information on most larger and mid-size firms can be found through a number of search engines.
- *Industry associations and trade groups.* All associations keep lists of their members, and most will sell these names and addresses. The great thing about these lists is that they are already somewhat qualified. That is, they are companies involved in a particular industry that are most likely active in that industry. If a particular association doesn't sell its list, you may be able to join the association to access the membership list—that's often one of the biggest reasons people join associations!
- *Trade magazines.* Most trade and business magazines produce an annual issue that ranks firms in their particular field. Many do annual product and supplier guides, which include the names, addresses, phone numbers, and other relevant information about businesses of interest to their particular industry.
- *Trade shows.* Every trade show I've attended has some method for generating a mailing list for people who pay for booths at the show. Typically the list is generated from information obtained at registration; sometimes the list is obtained by having people fill out information for a drawing, prize, or other giveaway. Often individual companies will sponsor a drawing at their booth in order to generate a lead list.

Depending on your type of business, booking a booth at a trade show may be an alternative. If that's too costly, simply attending a large trade show will enable you to collect hundreds of business cards and make as many industry contacts. Also don't overlook smaller regional and local trade shows. These shows are often very inexpensive, and buyers may have more time to spend with possible new sources of supply.

- *Mailing list brokers.* The worst way to generate leads is through completely unqualified lists, such as phone books, because you have no relationship with the prospect, no targeting criteria, and virtually no information about the lead. That's where list brokers come in. These people sell names of companies and individuals broken down by category. If you buy such a list, you still won't have a personal relationship with the lead, but at least you will know that selective criteria (e.g., the industry or location) have been applied in the process of assembling the list.

Many companies broker lists; check the *Yellow Pages* in the metro areas (check your local library for directories for distant cities). Most mailing lists are sold to businesses doing direct mail, not telemarketing or direct sales, although some can supply phone numbers on request. There are many different ways to buy the same names, so it's important to tell the broker exactly what you'd like. For example, you could buy the names of everyone who lives in a certain zip code. You could buy the names of subscribers to a particular magazine who live in a particular city. You could buy the names of computer manufacturing firms with sales between $10 million and $50 million located in California. You could also get mailing list brokers to merge lists for you and provide you with all of the names or only the names that show up twice. So, for example, you might be able to buy the names of business executives who subscribe to three particular magazines.

Mailing lists typically cost just a few cents per name, but there's usually a minimum charge of at

least several hundred dollars per list. The charge varies quite a bit from one mailing list broker to the next.

You can get mailing lists on disks or printed out on sheets of paper, on note cards (easy for phone contacting), or on pressure-sensitive labels (ready to be attached to envelopes).

Most mailing houses sell mailing lists for one-time use only. To prevent buyers from using a list more than once, lists are "seeded" with disguised addresses or phone numbers that actually lead back to the mailing list owner. In other words, if you try to use the list again, among the individuals receiving your "illegal" mailings will be the person who sold you the list for one-time use only. However, if a contact from a mailing list replies to your direct-mail piece or if you call a company on the list and qualify it as a prospect, then the mailing list has done its job. This contact now becomes part of your customer base and you can certainly contact them again.

Before spending a lot of money on a brokered list, keep in mind two things: (1) always test-contact a small list of names first to see how well they work for you; and (2) be aware that some mailing lists are sold and used often. Business executives and doctors, for example, are frequent requests—and the prospects on these lists are often deluged with calls and less inclined to be patient with yet another sales call.

Source #4: Network

Without a doubt, the best leads will be people you've had some previous contact with. Second-best are leads that someone you know refers to you.

The number-one networking method is getting referrals from current customers: The best way to get business is to get repeat business from your customers by finding out what their needs are and satisfying them. The next best way to get business is to get referrals from your satisfied customers, which you can also get by taking terrific care of them and by asking them for referrals.

Generally speaking, though, getting out and putting yourself in situations where you can meet potential leads or people who know potential leads is what networking is all about. Simply put, networking is introducing yourself and your business to people in situations other than a direct sales call. While you let others know a little about you and what you do, you're learning something about them and what they do. There is no pressure, because no one is making a sales call or having to sit through a presentation. Through casual conversation, you can easily discover whether this person is someone who is a potential buyer for your product or service, or whether they know someone who might be. At the same time, you'll discover whether the person you're talking to has something you'd like to buy, or that someone you know might like to buy. It's a give-and-take situation, and that's what makes it so nice. We'll talk more about how to network in Chapter 14. For now, let's review some of the places that offer great opportunities to gather business cards and network leads.

- *Industry trade shows and related events.* Particularly if you are selling nationally, consider joining or participating in a national trade association or professional group. At the least, you should find people like yourself you can network and brainstorm with. Trade and professional associations often have local chapters. You can find a listing of many professional associations on the World Wide Web at www.careercity.com.

- *Your local chamber of commerce or other business association.* Chambers can be costly to join if your business requires you to cover more than one city or town. At $200 to $300 each, joining chambers can add up. However, most chambers offer mixers for people who want to try them out before actually joining. They also hold events that you can sometimes attend on a trial basis—at a higher cost, naturally, than if you were a member.

- *Social clubs.* If you're selling products to local businesses, try to join or attend the activities of every relevant group you can. Some groups you may not be able to join as an individual may have some activities that are open to the public.

CHECKLIST

Ten Ways to Find Customers

❏ Source from the competition.

❏ Focus on the top 20 percent, the most active accounts in your industry.

❏ Mine ignored, neglected, forgotten segments of the marketplace.

❏ Develop an area of expertise and use it to cater to specialty accounts.

❏ Pull from qualified lists, such as industry and association membership lists.

❏ Network at business, trade, and social events.

❏ Get referrals from current customers.

❏ Set yourself up as an industry expert by teaching a class at your local community college.

❏ Shop for leads by reading newspapers, business journals, and so on.

❏ Ask your boss, industry people, clients, and other salespeople for help.

Also try to find people who belong to these associations and see if they will pass your cards around.

- *Fundraisers and other charity events.* Many businesses are proud to participate in fundraisers for good causes. Here's where you are likely to meet some of your community's movers and shakers!

- *Specialty business groups, such as Women In Business groups.* I found my banker (a man) at the monthly meeting of a local group of businesswomen. I'm not even sure that the by-laws of the group required members to be women. Regardless, even if you're a man, you can be a guest speaker or presenter at a function dedicated to promoting women in business. (A referral form to help you generate leads from a speaking engagement is included in the "Forms" appendix.) Consider other groups of minority business owners and physically challenged businesspeople—there are groups out there for all sorts of special situations these days. Or, consider whether you may have a friend who can invite you to some of the functions.

- *Alumni Associations.* Don't forget about the alumni or alumnae from your alma maters and other groups. Some sales reps have built their livelihood just selling to alumni or alumnae from their college or other schools. There is some immediate trust in this kind of sales situation. And by focusing all your efforts on one group, you are more likely to develop some positive word-of-mouth and to increase your chances of getting referrals.

- *Your local bookstore.* Bookstores are increasingly becoming community hubs, offering much more than books and perhaps a coffee shop. Most booksellers are finding it advantageous to attract customers by offering special events. Often, these events, while still designed to promote books, are tailored to special interests: finance seminars, home designs, weddings, and on and on. Keep abreast of your local bookstore's calendar of events to see if one is likely to draw a relevant crowd. Or consider running an event of your own! At many bookstores, you don't have to be an author to put together a program.

- *Your local community college.* Try teaching or taking a class. Many community colleges offer noncredit and credit classes in nonacademic subjects. They are also offering, at a modest cost, one-night lectures or day-long programs on business-related topics. If you are a financial planner, offer to teach a course—or try attending one. You'll meet people who already have a strong interest in what you have to offer—otherwise they would not be attending a financial seminar!

- *Your competition.* It might sound crazy, but a huge amount of business today is generated when one supplier who feels they either can't handle a job or aren't best suited for it recommends a competitor. This is happening more often as more sales reps focus on serving their customers as well as they can, even when it means recommending that some work may be better done by their competitors.

  For example, let's say a commercial printer does 90 percent of the printing work (primarily catalogs and product brochures) for a small manufacturing firm. The printer is then asked to print a hundred copies of a single-page party announcement. Because their presses are designed for longer runs, the commercial printer would have to charge the manufacturer three times what a small copy shop would charge. So the sales rep refers the job to a small copy shop. Although there are many small copy shops nearby, the sales rep refers the job to a particular shop because he recently met the sales rep and she spoke convincingly of the capabilities of her small shop.

  The lesson: When you meet sales reps from competing firms, don't shy away from them. Give them your card and tell them what kind of work your firm does best. (Cultivate detachment!)

- *Your Own Group.* What if you can't find an organization or club that suits your needs? Whether it's an investment club or a club to help

motivate salespeople from various industries, try starting one of your own!

We'll talk more about the finer details of networking in Chapter 14, but for now, let's continue with some other rules of finding leads.

Source #5: Become Media-Savvy

There are many reasons to keep abreast of what's happening in the local and national media. Obviously, you'll hear about industry trends and be better able to comment on them to your customers. You might even consider clipping relevant articles and adding them to your sales tool kit or sending them with a hand-written note to a client. Knowing what's happening in the news gives you a way to "break the ice" with a potential client and to establish some common bonds. You and your client are no different than everyone else who's talking about the latest scandal on Capitol Hill (but no opinions, please!). Newspaper articles, especially those in the business section, can be an additional source of sales leads. For selling to local businesses, pay particular attention to local business journals. They tend to focus on local firms. And the smaller the publication, the less likely you are to face competition from other firms calling the same buyer. For selling to national firms, you want to follow up with the trade press very carefully. For selling to individuals, keep track of the "Who's News" section of as many relevant publications as possible. That's where you'll find reports of promotions and job changes for those people in charge of making buying decisions.

Source #6: Ask for Help

Ask your boss, other salespeople, and people in the industry for ideas. As you experiment with finding leads, compare notes with others. It could be that in your particular situation the best method for finding prospects is very different from all the methods I just outlined! Find out what methods work for people in your situation. Don't be shy about asking salespeople at your firm or at similar firms what methods of finding leads is working for them.

Pruning Your Lead List

As you've seen, there's lots of information available. Perhaps too much! By now, you may feel a bit overwhelmed. Isn't there just one way to assemble a lead list?

The answer is no. There is no magic formula. There are many salespeople who have been successful at finding customers using just one method and there are even more who have been successful using several methods. There are no hard-and-fast rules about what is going to work for you. But generally, the more you personalize and target the lead, the more likely you are to be successful.

It's worth quite a bit of time to sort through the information you've gathered to put together as carefully pruned a list of prospects as you possibly can. The more time you spend refining and carefully targeting the people who are most likely to be interested in buying your product, the less time you will have to spend trying to sell to people who have no interest. That's why it's critical to spend lots of time qualifying your leads early in the sales process. (We'll show you how to do this in more detail in Chapters 5, 6, and 7, which talk about a process seasoned salespeople know as "precall planning.")

Here are some ways to work smarter, rather than harder, when compiling your lead list:

- *Ask yourself, are you selling a product that might be applicable for a broad range of businesses or consumers, such as printing services or paper products or office supplies?* If so, you should focus your effort on one customer segment at a time. For example, if you are selling office supplies you might want to put together a list of fifty banks to call, or if you are selling life insurance you may want to put together a list of fifty lawyers. This tactic has several benefits. First, it enables you to concentrate your efforts on learning the needs of a particular industry. You can prioritize your time by concentrating on that industry's trade shows and other networking events. Because your time and energy are dedicated to a single industry, your networking and referral possibilities increase. Then keep

KEY IDEAS

Fine-Tune Your Lead List

Although there's no single best way to get leads, generally speaking, the more personalized and targeted the lead is to your industry, the more likely you are to be successful converting leads to business.

careful track as you go through the sales process of how successful you are with each group that you are targeting. If a particular kind of customer or a particular kind of lead source proves promising, use that again and again until results fall off.

- *Test lead sources in a small way first to see if you get results.* What do I mean by testing? In Chapters 5 and 6, on precall planning, we talk about the importance of uncovering your prospect's needs by asking them a series of information-gathering questions. In Chapter 8 we talk about how those questions can be used to compile an information sheet on your prospect. Take some of the leads from a source through the list of questions outlined in those chapters. If you've prepared a customer information sheet on twenty decisionmakers (the number you should be able to contact in one day) from a lead list and feel you are getting nowhere, stop and evaluate what's going on. Do you need more practice going through the information-gathering process? Are you answering too many questions, giving too much information, spending too much time on your wants and needs, and not listening enough to the customer? (See Appendix D for a sample telephone script.)

  Or, are you listening enough and discovering that the product or service you're offering is truly irrelevant to the customer base? If you are getting a strong, certain message that the particular source of leads you're working is irrelevant or just not the best place to spend your time, move on to another source—quickly. Just be certain you aren't making that decision because you don't have a lot of experience working through the precall planning routine yet, or because you are "having a bad day." In the beginning, it's easy to get discouraged for either reason. When in doubt, be sure to consult with someone more experienced than you!

And who might that be? Well, it could be your sales manager, another salesperson, even a savvy friend. Or—
It could be the next person on the lead list! Tell the next lead you call that you're having this problem and you're wondering if they can help you find out what's wrong. At this point, you're not trying to sell him or her anything, you're just asking for a little honest feedback. Do they think their part of the marketplace wouldn't be interested in what you have to sell? You don't want to waste decisionmakers' valuable time! You might be surprised at what might happen when you honestly ask a decisionmaker for help.

- *Last, but not least, remember to step back and review your customer base and its needs.* In the process, you'll no doubt come up with some of your own creative ways to find new potential accounts.

CHECKLIST

Hone Your Selling Skills

You may not have much experience selling, but you can get some experience rather quickly by:

❑ Calling on a prospect who is a poor choice to see how you handle challenges that arise (If you make a mistake, who cares? They weren't likely to commit anyway, and at least you've learned to handle rejection. And, you never know, they might surprise you and buy— what a boost to your self-confidence!)

❑ Role-playing with friends and associates

❑ Accompanying a seasoned sales rep on several sales visits to learn and observe (Be open-minded, but don't be afraid to critique [internally] each visit— some experienced reps miss opportunities or welcome an opportunity to vent frustration to newcomers, and you want to avoid such negative baggage as you launch your career in sales.)

❑ Videotaping your sales pitch for self-analysis

CHAPTER 5

Precall Planning

KEY IDEAS

Knowledge Is Power—but Only If It's the Right Kind

It isn't how much you know that will close a sale—it's how much you know about your customer.

The number-one reason that salespeople fail is that they don't know enough about their customer. They give in to the temptation to list at length the benefits they perceive in the product they're selling, while forgetting the most important thing of all: *Customers don't want to be "sold." They want to decide for themselves to buy because a product or service fulfills a need they have.* Even highly motivated, energetic salespeople fall into traps when they make the following assumptions:

- A prospect is in the market for a product or service.
- A prospect has a need for that service.
- The client wants to hear all about a product's or service's function and benefits.
- The customer wants to hear why the salesperson thinks a product is great.
- The customer is only interested in price.
- The customer wants the best quality.
- The customer is interested in image or prestige.
- The customer wants to work with a large company.

I could go on, but I'm sure you're beginning to get the picture. To rephrase the statement made at the beginning of this section: *The number-one reason that salespeople fail is that they make assumptions about their clients that aren't true.*

The assumption can extend even to the most obvious issues. Far too many times I've witnessed a salesperson spend upward of an hour selling a product to a prospect, only to find out suddenly that the person wasn't even the decisionmaker! (Yes, plenty of people get their jollies from pretending to be the all-powerful decisionmaker when they may not even have a reason, desire, or the wherewithal to pass the information along to the key player.)

As a sales facilitator, it's your job to find out:

- How the customer defines value
- How the customer makes decisions
- What the customer sees as his or her biggest issue, challenge, or problem

- Whether the customer needs what you have to offer
- Why the customer should buy your product or service rather than a competitor's

The better prepared you are to understand the customer, the closer you are to making a sale, even before you begin. That's why what the experts call "precall planning" is so important.

What Is Precall Planning— and How Do You Do It?

The prefix *pre* indicates something that takes place before the word that follows it. Precall planning includes the prefix *pre* because, even before you call on clients, you can gather a lot of useful knowledge about their company or situation by asking the right questions—and getting some answers. The knowledge you gain in the precall process will position you for a successful sales call.

If you're a beginner at sales, you may think that "precall" planning refers to information gathered before you dial prospects and speak to them on the telephone. In sales lingo, however, the word *call* doesn't necessarily mean an actual phone conversation. It refers to the time when you are *calling on* prospects to ask for their business. You may have held many conversations with the prospect before the actual call or sales presentation occurs. It might be clearer to say pre–sales presentation information-gathering process" instead of using the term *precall planning*. But as they say on TV, how complicated is that? So in this book we'll stick to the industry standard, and use "precall planning" and "information-gathering process" interchangeably.

To be effective, precall planning should be done on a customer-by-customer basis, because every sales situation and every customer is unique. Every customer will have somewhat different concerns and put a different weight on the importance of different features and services. Some precall planning can be done on your own, before you introduce yourself to the client. For example, through industry sources, it's easy to discover what a company manufactures, how big their sales volume is, what type of products they manufacture and the price range, and how they've been growing the

KEY IDEAS

Prepare for a Sale Before You Meet with the Client

Even before you meet with clients, you can gather useful information about their situation and needs that will help position you for a successful sales call.

Customer Input Is Essential—*Before* You Pitch the Sale

The only person who can give you the information you need to know is the customer! Trying to answer important questions without customer input can lead you to make incorrect assumptions about what will interest the prospect in your product.

business. This kind of information will give you a good foundation for a preliminary evaluation of whether what you have to offer is even in the ballpark.

Much of the precall-planning process is actually gathering information directly from the prospect about needs. As I said earlier, a good salesperson avoids making assumptions.

If only the customer can provide you with the information you really need to have, then why not just arrange a meeting and make a presentation? There are three good reasons:

1. Precall planning can make you more knowledgeable about the issues your client *might* have.
2. Precall planning prepares you to ask the customer the right questions.
3. If at any time in the selling process an opportunity arises for you to prove your industry expertise, precall planning will ensure that you are the expert you claim to be. All knowledge can be helpful in the right place at the right time.

So, familiarize yourself with your own industry as part of the typical precall planning process, keep in touch with industry trends, and use them in preparing for a sales call. But it's wise to keep in mind the principle: Every customer is different, and what's happening in the industry may or may not be relevant to him or her!

For example, suppose a furniture store salesman had read that the birth rate is up, and more couples than ever are purchasing cribs. He also read a survey that showed traditional-style furniture is the most popular style of furniture being sold—a fact confirmed by his experience.

Now suppose you and your husband are in the market for contemporary-style dining room furniture. You walk into the furniture store, and the salesman approaches you. He walks right up and says, "Good evening, thanks for visiting the store." So far, so good, right? Next he says, "Let me tell you all about our traditional-style baby cribs."

Sounds pretty ridiculous, right? Yet this is what salespeople do every day when speaking to potential new clients. They start pitching what they think the client wants to hear, rather than finding out what the client's needs are.

You may understand why his response to seeing you and your husband enter the furniture store makes sense to him. But, from the customer's point of view, it makes no sense at all.

This scenario isn't much different than a salesperson beginning a sales call with "Our new industrial engine has 275 horsepower," before finding out whether the customer is looking for such a large engine—or even an engine at all. Perhaps the company is looking for a less powerful engine, or a widget instead of an engine. Perhaps the company is looking to buy a widget from you not because it needs widgets—it has a warehouse full of them—but it's trying to upgrade its image. This company wants to tell its customers that it uses only top-grade, brand-name widgets in its newest machine.

More Benefits to the Information-Gathering Process

For any sales presentation to make sense, the salesperson must have critical information about the prospect's needs that can only be obtained from the customer. Involving the prospect in the precall-planning process has additional benefits as well.

Asking questions causes customers to invest their time and energy in the sale—rather, the "buy." Because they have invested what they regard as one of their most precious commodities (time), they will take your proposal much more seriously. Emotionally, if for no other reason, they will want to see your proposal succeed! To put it even more simply, *they will want to buy*.

To summarize, by asking customers for information, you accomplish the following:

- Involve them in the planning process.
- Commit their energy to working with you to discover a solution to their needs.
- Turn what might otherwise appear to be a pushy sales call into a genuine exploration of the customers' needs.

Use Industry Knowledge to Ask Appropriate Questions

Knowing what's going on in your industry and how it might affect a particular customer is useful, even necessary, for success in sales. The *real* benefit of precall planning is that it sets you up to ask the right questions so you can become an expert on your customer.

Learn to Focus on the Prospect's Needs

Consider the following sales pitches and how they negatively impact a potential sale:

- "Our catering firm does upscale weddings and has worked with many celebrities." What if the customer is a middle-class individual looking to throw a modestly priced fortieth birthday party?

- "We are the largest provider of inexpensive widgets, mass-marketing them to thousands of factories internationally." What if the company being pitched needs someone who can custom-manufacture a widget to the exacting standards of a proprietary design?

Exercise: On a sheet of lined paper, write down ten or more good reasons to buy your product or service. Leave space between each reason. Beneath each reason to buy, list one or two reasons your pitch might turn off a customer in a specific situation.

A great way to show decisionmakers that you are truly interested in hearing about their business is to let them know up-front that you aren't making a sales call, rather you're looking for information. A good way to put this is to tell them (assuming they're a new prospect) that you've never spoken to them before, and that being new in the industry (or the territory, etc.), you would like to learn more about what they do. Once you have a good understanding of their business, there might be some way you can help them, although at this point you're not certain.

If they say they are not interested in buying anything right up-front, ask them whether they'd be willing to spend a few minutes of their time helping to educate you by explaining what they do. Many people are surprisingly willing to meet with or talk to you when a request is phrased this way.

Many times, appointments obtained this way have surprising results. Sometimes prospects change their minds and express an interest in doing business with you, even though they already told you they weren't interested. After you've questioned them about their needs, it may become apparent to them that some of their needs aren't being met—at least, not as thoroughly as they'd like. Or they may ask you for information about what you do, and express an interest in the possibility of doing business with you at a later date. And, if they don't want to or can't do business with you at the present time, you may be surprised to find that, once they've spent some time with you, they'll recommend you to other people—even though they have bought nothing from you themselves!

An information-gathering meeting or approach has another benefit that can help you sell in the future. No salesperson is perfect, and even satisfactory relationships with providers may worsen at some point. Whether a crisis happens and they become disenchanted with their current provider, or an opportunity to bid arrives when the current provider's contract is up for renewal, you'll have a head start. You won't be "cold calling" the client because you'll already have a relationship with them.

As we saw when we explored the furniture store vignette, when you plan for a sales call, there are always two points of view to consider: yours and the customer's. There's the customer's agenda, and there's your agenda. These two agendas will become apparent once you've gathered a certain amount of information about the client. In the next chapter, we'll cover the precall information-gathering process in more detail.

Plant Seeds Every Day.

Prospecting is a big key to your success. In your early days of selling you will have all day, every day, to prospect. As you become more experienced, you will tend to spend more time with your customer base, but this leaves less time for prospecting. That's the root of the problem. If you look at your success today, it is a direct result of the good prospecting you did six months ago. The question now is: What are you doing today to make sure that business is great six months from now? The answer: Plant seeds every day. No matter how busy or great business is today, to attain consistently high sales results you must engage in prospecting activities daily. Your efforts may shift over time, but regardless, you must do something every day toward new business development. Use the methods most effective for you—cold calls, warm calls, networking, speaking, writing. Get out there, be proactive, and set up your future by planting seeds today.

Let Go of Tactics and Develop Personal Judgment Skills.

Using personal judgment skills means trusting yourself to say the right thing, at the right time, in the right way. Personal judgment skills come from knowing your products or services inside out, doing an accurate assessment of your potential client, and then answering directly how your product or service can link the two. With Customer-Focused Selling you have to let go of the need for manipulation, and trust the process of working with your customer. Step one is to let go of the crutches and believe in yourself. Step two is understanding that the customer wants that degree of true connection. And step three is to practice, practice, practice. Sharp personal judgment skills come from the day-to-day experiences of letting go of tactics and replacing them with outstanding customer focus.

Manage the Sales Process with Next Steps.

You know it's your job to manage the sales process, but how often do you really feel like you're in the driver's seat? The desired answer should be that you feel you're always in control. Managing the Customer-Focused Selling process means knowing exactly where you stand at all times and what it will take to advance the sale. The best way to stay in control is to make sure you establish "next steps" at the close of every interaction. Whether it's a phone call, a face-to-face meeting, E-mail, or a letter . . . ALWAYS clearly state or determine next steps. Focus on defining a summary of the sales status, and a statement of what each party will do next. By managing the sales process you eliminate misconceptions, misunderstandings, and stalled sales. In effect you are collaboratively agreeing to move the process ahead by agreeing on next steps!

CHAPTER 6

Uncovering the Prospect's Agenda

Precall planning is both industry and customer specific, so only you can know which questions are appropriate for your clients. This chapter covers a typical information-gathering approach in depth, so you have a method to work with and refine.

Because I was a busy professional with multiple responsibilities, I did not always find it easy to remember to stay on track during telephone conversations with buyers. When you've got a lot on your mind, it's easy to lose focus and forget to ask key questions. I'm sure I'm not alone! After a couple of such experiences, I was able to gather information much more efficiently, plus jump-start the sales process and bond with the prospect more readily thanks to a customer information sheet (CIS), custom-designed for my needs.

Designing the Customer Information Sheet

My CIS (see following page) may look complicated to an outsider, but for me the design made perfect sense, giving me the client's history at a glance. In this next section, I'll cover the careful process that I went through to design my sheet—and my sales campaign. That way, you'll be better able to undertake the process of designing one of your own to meet your (and your customer's) needs. Appendix E contains sample precall-planning sheets.

Precall planning can be broken down into three parts. The checklists outline what information should be covered in each category.

Part 1: General Information

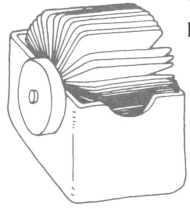

General information is all of the obvious data that you might put in a Rolodex—your basic contact information. Start by recording general company information, the sort found on most business cards. If the business card or other source for the lead does not have this information, most of the data can be obtained by calling the company receptionist.

❑ Date
❑ Company name
❑ Company address (P.O. Box, Street, City, State, Zip)

CUSTOMER INFORMATION SHEET

CUSTOMER INFORMATION SHEET   AE _____

Account Name: _____ Type of Business _____
Address: _____
Phone Number: _____ Web Site: _____ E-mail: _____
Fax: _____ Referred By: _____ Date _____

<table>
<tr><th>KEY PERSONNEL</th><th>COMMENT</th></tr>
</table>

Owner: _____   _____
Address: _____   Phone #: _____
Agency: _____   _____
Address: _____   Phone #: _____
Media Planner: _____   _____
Address: _____   Phone #: _____
Media Buyer: _____   _____
Address: _____   Phone #: _____
Other: _____   _____

ADVERTISING HISTORY

TYPE	SIZE	DATE	WHERE	COST
1c 2c 4c 0c	_____	_____	_____	_____
1c 2c 4c 0c	_____	_____	_____	_____

Promo #1 _____   Press Release: _____   Our Goal for This Client: _____
Phone Call _____   About   _____
Media Kit _____   Press Release: _____   _____
  Rate Card   About   _____
  Folder   Press Release: _____   _____
  Testimonials   About _____   _____
  Map   Notepad w/ logo
  Circulation Director (this would be a promotional   Promo Possibilities:
  Folder   "freebie") _____   _____ Sweepstakes Other: _____
  Cover   Other: _____   _____ Bridal Fair   _____
  Publisher's Letter   _____   _____ Comp Issues   _____
  Business Card   _____   _____ Contest   _____
  Contract   _____   _____ Party   _____
Post Card #1 _____   Thank-You _____   _____ Merchandise
Post Card #2 _____   Complimentary issue _____

Date	Action Taken	Results/Comments	Follow-up

❑ Company telephone number
❑ Fax number
❑ E-mail address
❑ Web site address
❑ Type of business
❑ Referred by

Here are some additional points about a few of these categories. The *date* should list the date the lead became active. Later, when you review account progress, or perhaps need to purge some data, knowing when you started prospecting will come in handy.

When recording the *company name*, make an effort to list it completely and correctly! Don't forget the Inc. or Ltd., and confirm unusual spacings or spellings. First impressions count in correspondence, and this will save you from having to verify the information later.

Unless it's an extremely large corporation, the type of business should be pretty obvious. However, you can customize this item on the header section to suit your particular needs. For example, you may be in a business where you divide your clients by category. A sales rep for a general interest magazine may identify each customer according to beauty, fashion, catering, home and garden, travel, health, restaurant, accounts, and so on. Another sales rep might find it useful to identify the prospect by size—small, medium, large—another, by territory.

It's also helpful to note where the lead came from—*referred by*. Was it a cold call from the phone book, a newspaper, or some other listing? Was it a referral from a friend, an existing customer, or another vendor or service provider? Or was it an internal referral from someone at the company? Perhaps you heard of the company through a chamber of commerce meeting or a trade show. Maybe you met someone from the company at a Women In Business networking seminar. Whatever the source, writing it down will do two things. *First, it will remind you to think about how you can leverage this information.* Suppose you met the owner of a company at a networking seminar. Now, when you call on that

person, you've already met her, so it's no longer a cold call. Plus, since you both attended the same function, you already have something in common. If it was a business function, by reminding your prospect that that's where you met, you'll also be reminding her that you are "out in the field," obviously on top of things in your industry. The function itself can provide an "icebreaker" when you call that person or, if you get an appointment, meet with her.

If the referral was from a mutual acquaintance, many of the same benefits apply. In addition, a referral, while not exactly an endorsement, implies that the mutual acquaintance at least thinks that it would be a good idea for the two of you to talk.

Second, it will enable you to track the success of a variety of sources for leads. Selling is all about good time-management skills. In the beginning, while you are building a "list" (sales lingo for a list of prospects), you won't know which sources will supply the best leads and which sources are marginal. As you "work your leads" and note the source of the lead, you'll get a good idea of which leads your time is best spent pursuing.

Part 2: Key Players

Next, you'll want to identify the key players in the organization who are involved in making the decision to buy.

- ❑ Name
- ❑ Title
- ❑ Address
- ❑ Phone number
- ❑ E-mail
- ❑ Responsible for

Some companies may have a purchasing agent who rules as a minor god and sole decisionmaker. In today's very complicated marketplace, however, the decisionmaking is often divided among several people—such as the president, the vice-president, the purchasing agent or buyer, the department head, the production manager, the office manager, the quality control manager, the head of marketing, the director of promotion, the head of customer service.

A Creative Use for Business Cards

A successful sales rep designed her customer information sheet with a blank, business-card square in the upper left-hand corner. Then she could staple or tape her contact's business card right on her tracking sheet for easy reference.

KEY IDEAS

Don't Be Fooled by Titles

Titles vary from company to company, and there is often a disconnection between what the title says and what level of authority the person really has over a buying decision. If you don't already know, it's worth asking the receptionist who it is that handles buying what you have to sell. You can then begin to do some preliminary work qualifying the decisionmakers by calling their administrative assistants.

As you are referred up the totem pole and speak to people who appear to be decisionmakers or connected to them, try to get a sense of their level of authority. Does he have responsibility for a budget? Or does he have responsibility for results? The higher up you can reach, the better off you are! Make sure you determine what the person does, and look for clues for an authorized decisionmaker. You'll qualify the key players further in a face-to-face interview, but for now, you need to ask questions to determine which contacts are key players and how to contact them.

And, by the way, don't forget about the "key people" who may not make decisions, but who can put you in touch with those who can. *It doesn't hurt to get to know and cultivate the key player's assistant(s).* When people are difficult to talk to—as key decisionmakers often are—the only way you may be able to get a telephone conference or face-to-face meeting is by cultivating a positive relationship with other people inside the organization who can "sell" the key player on your behalf—or, at least, sell him or her on holding a telephone conversation with you.

Part 3: Portrait of the Business

Now that you have a skeleton portrait of the business, it's important to round out your understanding of the customer's situation. Ideally, this section of the task will lead you to identify the customer's key issues—the desires, problems, and needs that make the prospect a candidate for your product or service.

Most people, no matter how pressed for time, are happy to tell you what they do. And that's great, because in order to serve prospects best, the more you know, the better.

So, this third step of the information-gathering process is to draft a list of thoughtful questions to ask the prospect. Here are a few ideas.

❑ What product or service does the prospect supply?

❑ How does the company position itself in the marketplace? What customers is it trying to reach?

❑ How competitive is the company's marketplace right now? And who is their competition?

❑ What are the biggest issues, challenges, or problems being faced now?

❑ What changes and trends in the industry are impacting the prospect's business?

❑ How has the company addressed these problems/issues?

❑ Were the solutions tried successful? Is there any room for improvement?

❑ What would help the prospect to improve their productivity or market penetration or whatever it is they're trying to do?

❑ What aspects of the product or service provided by a company like yours would the prospect find useful?

❑ Why would the prospect buy from one company as opposed to another?

❑ Has the prospect thought about ways a product or service like yours could better position the company in the marketplace?

❑ (Picking up on the prospect's concerns/issues) If there were a better way to [address the prospect's needs], would the prospect be interested in hearing about it?

❑ What is the average size of a contract the decisionmaker offers a company like yours? (What are they spending currently on widgets?)

❑ What is the company getting for the money spent? How much or what kind of service or "extras" is the company getting from its current supplier (in addition to the widgets)?

❑ What is the buying cycle? (When are decisions to buy made? When is the next contract up for renewal?)

❑ Would the company decisionmakers be interested in hearing at a future date what business opportunities your product or service can create for them?

❑ May you set an appointment now?

❑ If not, would there be a better time to touch base with them again?

DIALOGUE BOX

Verifying a Title

Here's a sample dialogue.

Ms. Prospect's administrative assistant: Jane Beder speaking.

You: Hi, Jane Beder. I'm wondering if you can help me. I understand you're Ms. Prospect's assistant?

Jane Beder: That's right.

You: Well, I was told to speak to Ms. Prospect about a matter involving buying widgets. But I'm not sure that she's the right person to speak to. Could you tell me what Ms. Prospect is in charge of?

Jane Beder: Ms. Prospect designs our widget specifications.

You: I see. Do you know who makes decisions about buying widgets?

Jane Beder: I'm not certain, but I believe Mr. Purchase is in charge of that.

You: Thanks so much. I really appreciate your time, Jane. Would it be possible for you to transfer me to Mr. Purchase's assistant? Or do you by any chance have the number, so I can dial directly?"

Get the Customer to Fantasize an Ideal Scenario

By asking the customer to "dream," you encourage him to reveal his biggest desire and give you the opportunity to fulfill it. Try to get the client to complete this sentence: "If only ——— were solved, then I'd be all set." Or, "In the best of all possible worlds, if I had my druthers, I'd do it like this:———."

These questions are designed to help you in the early stages of preparing for the sale. They aren't meant to be recited from a sheet as though you were a telemarketer conducting a survey. Although, I believe typing them on a sheet and photocopying the "questionnaire" is essential. They are meant to be asked in a conversational tone, with an air of genuine interest in your client. Having them in front of you while you are talking to the prospect will help you maintain control of the conversation. It's okay to paraphrase the questions, rather than read them directly from the sheet. It's okay to mix them up as you chat with the client. You may even find you need to stretch some of the questions over one or more conversations.

The questions on this part of the form can also be incorporated into a meeting. You can preface your remarks with, "I just want to make sure I understand your goals here. In our last conversation you said you were having a problem with quality control? Can you tell me more about that?" By paraphrasing the questions on your CIS form at a meeting with your contact and perhaps other members of the prospect's company, you remind them why they set up the meeting with you in the first place. Because they have a problem to solve.

Develop "Second Sight"

As you move through the selling process, you'll find many opportunities to refine your understanding of the prospect's situation. So filling out a customer information sheet is never a "done deal." Your goal here is to always keep the door open so you can call, revisit, or pitch the prospect again. Over time, the information-gathering approach allows your picture of the prospect to become more fully rounded and deeper, positioning you to get at hidden reasons for buying.

Sometimes prospects hide their true interest in a product or service because revealing their needs to a salesperson makes them feel vulnerable. This can make it difficult to accurately assess whether the prospects mean it when they say they're interested or not interested.

TIPS FOR CREATING GOOD QUESTIONS

Of course, the questions you ask can and should be customized for your industry. In concocting your own list of suitable questions, consider the following:

❏ *Look at the "big picture."* Consider what you know about the industry. Is it a mature industry? A new industry? A changing industry? In what ways is the industry changing? Is the industry faced with new regulations or new technology? Do you hear about the industry in the news often? Rarely? Why? Why not? By thinking about these questions, you'll identify potential key issues to address with the prospective client.

❏ *Relate the "big picture" to your prospect's particular situation.* Looking at your assessment of the industry, how does all this impact your prospective client? Is it causing the client to reexamine areas of her business? Change the size of the work force? Invest in specific areas of the business? Take greater risks? Reduce risks? Spend more? Spend less? This question will help you transition from the big picture to the prospective client's specific situation and understand how the industry climate is impacting the client.

❏ *Evaluate the prospect's competition.* How stiff is the company's competition? Think about what you know, what you've observed, and what you've read. How has the client positioned his company in the marketplace with respect to pricing? Is the company the most expensive, the least expensive, or somewhere in the middle? What else is the competition doing? Is the competition offering something in addition to the basic product to boost its competitiveness in the client's marketplace? What kind of added value are they offering? Incentives? Promotions? What is driving the competitive nature of the company: the industry or the consumer? You are uniquely positioned to look at the competition and better understand how the prospect sees the competition. Is he on the mark, or has he missed the boat? Start thinking about how you can help!

❏ *Discover what challenges the prospect's business faces.* Every business faces a challenge. What is the challenge for your prospect's business? Are the issues related to profit, people, time, technology, equipment, or a combination? Think about the prospective client's day-to-day responsibilities. Look at all the possibilities, including low margins and company inefficiencies. Jot down what you see as the company's biggest industry issues, challenges, or problems.

❏ *Look for underlying psychological reasons for buying.* Despite a prospect's claim to the contrary, she may decide to buy a product for purely emotional reasons. Most people, though, feel a bit sheepish admitting that they are spending money because they want to boost their ego, make friends in the marketplace, or for any of a hundred other illogical reasons. With a little persistence, you can usually uncover these profound yet seemingly invisible needs!

When you gain a little field experience, you'll find out that clients rarely make a logical decision to buy. They buy to fulfill emotional wants and desires. For example, a bridal gown designer might create an extreme ad campaign featuring waiflike models with deer antlers on their heads, dressed in bridal gowns. Why? Most brides I know don't want to walk down the aisle looking like waifs dressed in deer antlers and bridal gowns. Rather, it's because the designer has some fantasy of being an avant-garde designer from a high-end European couture house, even though he's actually Brooklyn born and raised.

Similarly, when a customer buys a security alarm system, she might "buy" the hardware, but what she really wants is the result, peace of mind. When a customer buys a retirement investment plan, he might buy stocks, bonds, and insurance, but what he really wants is a secure source of income at a later date. Look at your product or service: Ask the customer what results they really care about. Give yourself room to explore potentially irrational, but very powerful—often *the* most powerful—motivators to buy.

Stay Powerful: Refuse to Give the Prospect a Reason to Buy

The ultimate question in every buyer's mind is, Why should I buy your product? You need to know the answer in advance! However, the reason you need to know the benefits of your product in advance is *not* because you are going to tell prospects about your product or service's features or benefits at this stage. No, you are going to repress any urge to do anything other than ask them about their point of view, and listen carefully to their answers! Now, while you are filling out your info sheet is not the time to talk about your company.

Is your product faster, bigger, smaller, or smarter? Do you offer a different approach to an old problem? Do you customize and tailor to meet the specific needs of your customers? Figure out the distinguishing factors and then use the information to find out your fit in the marketplace! Are you priced high, low, or right in the middle? Do you offer more, less, or the same? Do you look

But what if the customer starts asking you questions? Resist answering them! Instead, ask her a question in return. For example, suppose the prospect asks, "What's your manufacturing turnaround time?" An inappropriate response would be, "Ten days." An appropriate response would be, "Is turnaround time important to you? What kind of turn-around time do you need?"

Suppose she asks, "What are the features your product offers?" A possible response would be, "What features would be most useful to your company?" If she presses you for details, you can tell her quite honestly: "Our company believes that the needs of the client are paramount. We offer more than just a [feature, product, whatever the prospect is pressing you for further information about]; we offer a way to achieve your goals. And the best way to help you achieve your goal is to find out as much as we can about your company and its needs, so we can come up with the best solution for you." That way the conversation stays focused on the prospect's needs.

Exercise: Practice answering questions with questions. Ask a friend to help, or make it a game that you play with your children. See how long you can go before either one of you breaks down!

like your competition? Or very different? Once you've identified who you are in relation to your competitors, everything can be turned into a positive. For example, if your company is small, you might ask the prospect if he likes to work with companies that offer the advantage of great flexibility; if your company is large, you can ask if working with a company that offers a wealth of resources would be beneficial for him.

But resist pointing out that your company is large, small, or anything else at this stage! Keep the conversation focused on the customer's needs—not on what you have to offer.

Although the precall-planning and information-gathering process may seem time-consuming and tedious, there is no better foundation for a sale. If you were building a house, you'd want your house to rest on a solid foundation. The same is true for sales! Think of information gathering as your foundation for selling. Take the time—an hour, two hours, or two days, whatever it takes—to build a strong foundation with the client right from the start. A firm foundation with your client will help you overcome hurricanes and earthquakes in the future.

Let Your Enthusiasm Show.

Letting your enthusiasm show doesn't mean jumping up and down with a big toothy grin in your customer's office. It does mean letting them see how much you care. Do you love what you do? Would you do it for free? Is it fun? Do you get excited when you uncover your customer's problems and solve them with your product or service? Enthusiasm comes from passion about what you do, what you represent, and how you impact your customers. Customer-Focused Selling lets you show your customers that you "hear them," understand them, can help them, and like doing it! Enjoy, and let them see the enthusiasm in your work.

Be a Student of the World.

In sales you should strive to be a good communicator and to develop the ability to connect with others. The more you are aware of the world around you, the better you will reach your customers on diverse levels. When was the last time you took a field trip to your local library and walked from aisle to aisle with no specific book in mind? Take the time to wander into the world of books, to journey into unknown areas, to explore new hobbies. Whatever your interests, be they in science, psychology, travel, business, self-development, or spirituality, you are best served by expanding your outlook. You may be in sales, but you don't sell to companies, you sell to people in companies. People relate to people. Be a student of the world and you will grow in your ability to relate to others on different planes, in different ways, and in different worlds.

Always Be Positive.

Being in sales, you are likely a "people person" and are out in the business world all day long. This provides a great opportunity to touch many people in positive ways. Take this part of your job very seriously because your words can have great impact. Positive words can build an opportunity; negative words can leave harmful debris. Most importantly, the way you operate day-to-day speaks volumes about your character and who you really are. You can't be a louse one minute and a charmer the next and expect to be successful. Commit yourself to living with the highest integrity every day. Respect your profession, respect others, and always be positive.

CHAPTER 7

Setting Your Agenda for the Client

O nce you have a clear picture of the prospect's key issue(s), your next step is to evaluate the information you've gathered to find out whether you can and should do business with the prospect.

Step 1: Evaluating the Client's Situation

Evaluating the information you have involves asking four questions:

1. Who are the decisionmaker(s)?
2. What are the client's needs?
3. Does the client have a sufficient budget to address the problems identified?
4. When would the decisionmaker(s) be able to make a decision to buy?

If you can answer these questions in a positive fashion, then you can move on to the next step: Figuring out the best way to help them. If you don't have enough information, you need to go back to the beginning of the precall-planning process, gather some information, and fill in the blanks. So you don't waste time and energy, you need to pay particular attention to how big a problem the prospect has and how motivated he or she is to do something about it. Most likely, you chose to invest time in gathering information about this company because you had some sense that it was a likely prospect for the service or product you represent. But sometimes, after you've gotten to this point, you realize that the company truly isn't a great prospect. Although you don't want to give up altogether, you may want to pursue this particular company less vigorously and go after other prospects on the list that show more promise. For example, if the decisionmaker says there's a problem, but has no budget to fix it—that isn't going to work, is it?

Nor do you want to "sell" to someone who can't pay for the sale. Occasionally, a prospect will tell you up-front he just doesn't have the money to buy. Sometimes this is true, and you need to respect the prospect's honesty. Sometimes this is a smokescreen, a white

lie designed to ward off a sales call. However, if the information you've gathered about the prospect indicates the company does have the means to consider your solution, whether he's admitted it to you or not, you may decide to continue the pursuit.

Step 2: What Solution Can You Offer?

If you are ready to continue, now is the time to think about how your product or service can help the prospect. Ask yourself:

1. How can my product or service help this company directly within their business?
2. How can my product or service help them in their marketplace?
3. What business results can my product or service create for this client?

To save time, it might be helpful to create a checklist of benefits to remind yourself of possible options. This client is looking for:

❑ Increased efficiency
❑ Increased sales
❑ Cost reduction
❑ Better image
❑ Customer retention
❑ More upscale customers
❑ Expansion of the customer base
❑ A different customer base
❑ Better service from a vendor
❑ Added value (extra services beyond the product or service being bought, such as working with you to put on a promotion or special event, free lead lists, promotional merchandise)
❑ Better positioning in the marketplace
❑ Support so it can meet its competitor head-to-head
❑ Marketplace knowledge
❑ Corporate identity

You Are Worth What You Charge

Sometimes there are other reasons besides income that make you feel it would be valuable to work with a particular prospect. For example, you might feel that the company is so prestigious, selling to it would give *you* a better position in the marketplace. Or perhaps the prospect is well connected and selling to him or her would lead to other sales. These reasons can motivate you as the salesperson, but they don't motivate the buyer! Whatever reason you'd like to get this prospect to become your client is secondary to whether the customer has the means—the need and the funds—to buy your solution! Don't fall into the trap of "selling at any cost." You need to get a fair price for the service you provide.

ATTITUDE ADJUSTMENT

Affirm Your Uniqueness

Ask yourself, Why are you offering the best solution? There are a lot of options out there today, but there's only one you. Think about how and why you are uniquely qualified as the best solution for this prospective client. Why are you better? Jot down five to seven reasons, and look at them. Are you detail oriented, customer focused, honest, experienced, dedicated, committed, knowledgeable, ethical? Most likely you are a great combination of these qualities, so you should take credit for what you do well. This is often the reason buyers decide to work with you. Identify your strengths, and understand why these are the reasons you're the best solution!

- ❏ Better production timing
- ❏ Quality (i.e., parts or systems that break down less often)
- ❏ Repair service twenty-four hours a day
- ❏ Educational support to know how to use the product/service you're selling

It shouldn't be hard to figure out what the customer needs after you've asked all of those questions during the precall analysis stage!

Step 3: Set a Goal for the Client

Clients will not set goals for how much business you can do with them. That's your job. So your next step is simple: Set a specific goal for the client.

What would you like this client to buy from you?
How much would you like to see them spend?

Make sure your projections are realistic; that is, within this company's means and answering the needs outlined earlier.

Step 4: Outline the Actions You Need to Take to Reach the Goal

Ask yourself what steps you can take to achieve your goal.

- Do you need to examine your own positioning a little more?
- Do you need to talk to some folks inside your own company before you proceed?
- Do you need to set a face-to-face meeting with the decision-maker?
- Do you need to come up with a proposal?
- Do you need to write a follow-up letter?
- Can you ask for an interim commitment?

Remember, you are in control! It's up to you to make it happen!

CHAPTER 8

Essential
Record Keeping

I magine what it's going to be like when you are a successful salesperson with hundreds of small-to-medium clients. Or, picture yourself as a salesperson involved in managing just one or two major contracts for multimillion-dollar corporations and interacting with twenty or more individuals at each corporation, each of whom is the head of a department with a specific expertise and list of responsibilities.

At the start of any given business day, the phone rings. On the other end could be any one of those people you deal with, at any company, at any phase of the selling process, asking you any type of question. Or, it might be a prospect you have been trying to connect with, but haven't managed to speak to yet. Or maybe the phone doesn't ring at all, so it's up to you to make a phone call. You need to make sure you call someone you haven't called yet, or haven't called lately. Or, perhaps you need to follow up on a call someone made to you yesterday or the day before.

Maybe you are one of the rare individuals who remembers everyone you've ever spoken to and the last conversation you had with them in great detail. These people do exist. The wife of a dean at a college I attended was famous for putting a name to a face after a single meeting. However, in the twenty-two years since I attended one of her garden parties, I have yet to meet another person who could make that claim. Like me and most people out there, you're probably going to need some help keeping all of your clients, prospects, companies, and your history with them, straight.

Believe me, you need a record-keeping system.

Characteristics of a Good Record-Keeping System

It's up to you to determine what the most relevant information is for your particular business. But here are some basic items any salesperson would find helpful to have handy:

❑ A one-page customer information sheet (CIS) containing basic information about the prospect or client, such as the company name, address, and phone number; the names and phone numbers of key management personnel or decisionmakers; and the history of the account

- ❏ A "log" noting your attempts to contact the customer, and what actions, if any, those contacts resulted in (This can begin at the bottom or on the back of the CIS if there's room and can expand to a separate sheet. The log should be very simple, a place for the date of contact and a corresponding box for you to record actions taken, results, and what follow-up is needed.)
- ❏ Copies of any recent correspondence or proposals that are still pending
- ❏ Copies of the last sales contract (if you've sold them something)

In sum, your record-keeping system should:

- • Give you access to vital information within a few seconds
- • Be easy to update, unobtrusively, while you're talking on the phone, or possibly even while you're holding a meeting
- • Be easy to "purge" when certain information is no longer needed

How Keeping Good Records Empowers You

Business etiquette requires most people to introduce themselves at the start of a conversation by giving their name, their company, and their title and/or department. If you're lucky, when a prospect or client calls you, you'll at least have this bare-bones introduction to jog your memory. Although these basic "stats" are helpful, there are many more things that it would be useful for you to know at the start of any sales conversation. Assuming that you have already gathered some information on the client, and that you keep that information in a system that allows you to access it easily, you'll be able to listen to a bare-bones

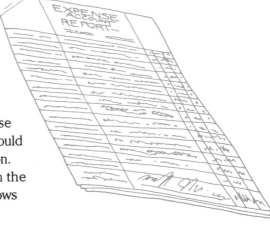

introduction and, in little more than the time it takes to return a greeting, know the following:

- To whom you're speaking
- What the title or position in the company signifies
- Who makes the buying decision in that company
- What the company does
- What reasons the company might have for buying from you
- What the budget is for buying
- Whether there is a relationship with a competitor of yours
- What promotions or parts of the tool kit have been received
- What has been purchased from you, or what you want the client to buy
- When the last contact was made with this company or individual
- What happened the last time you contacted the company

Knowing these things about your client or potential customer places you in a position of power—to help your client get more business (through selling them something they need) or to provide the best service to a client who has already bought something from you. Doesn't the idea of an easy-to-access prospect sheet make you feel more confident answering the phone already?

Paper Record Systems

Just as important as organizing the *ingredients* of your sales tool kit is organizing the records you'll generate on a day-to-day basis as you contact, follow up, sell to, and service clients and potential clients.

Systems for keeping records are as varied as the salespeople who use them. I have seen everything from elaborate binders with preprinted forms to slots in which the salesperson placed cards with different tasks. The cards could be moved around and priorities changed. Samples are included in Appendix F. I knew one salesman who depended solely on a desk blotter–size calendar on which he noted calls and visits to be made. (In my opinion, this isn't a very useful method, since even on such a large calendar, there's only room enough for about five notations—and no means of easily searching for prior contacts or other relevant client information.) Another seasoned sales professional I knew used alphabetized index cards for storing client contact information.

Ultimately, only you can decide what method suits you best, but the one I have found most useful was suggested by a sales rep for a regional magazine. I asked my friend how easy it had been for her to make the transition from a nonsales job to her first sales job. Her reply: "Difficult, until another salesperson in the company gave me a way to organize my leads and showed me how to work the system."

Like all great techniques, her method of organizing was truly simple. She purchased a classic three-ring binder with alphabetized dividers. She hole-punched a general client information sheet and any follow-up correspondence relating to the client and inserted it behind the appropriate tab. With all of her clients in alphabetical order, she could easily grab the notebook (which she always kept handy) and quickly flip to a specific company's information in a second. If the client list grew too large to fit in one notebook, the alphabetized tabs could be divided between two or more notebooks, with A–G in notebook 1, and H–O in notebook 2, and so on.

With all of the leads organized and in one place, it was easy for her to start at the beginning of her notebook and work her way through to the end in alphabetical order. Each week she would go through the book from start to finish, skipping those prospects who were on hold and attending to those who needed contact. In this way, she could be sure to cover all of her list in an organized fashion and didn't have to be concerned about overlooking someone.

If you are in a business that requires you to go out on the road, the alphabetized binder is helpful because you can take it with you—it's the ultimate portable record-keeping system! If you travel in various regions or "sales territories," you may find it helpful to create a binder for each territory and alphabetize your leads within each regional notebook. That way, you won't waste time trying to figure out that a prospect in southwestern

KEY IDEAS

Monitor for Balance

Far from being a waste of time, keeping records is one of the best ways to monitor your progress. If you suspect you're taking too much time away from direct client contact to do paperwork, try monitoring the way you spend your time for one week. Each day, list the hours spent on nonclient contact activities at the top of the page. Then list direct client contact activities, such as phone calls and meetings, at the bottom of the page. Use the results of your experiment to adjust your allotment of time spent on paperwork or client contact, depending on what you find and what you want to be doing. Client contact is, of course, the most important but the paperwork can't be ignored!

Pennsylvania isn't relevant on the day you are driving around northeastern Pennsylvania.

As your history with a prospect or client grows, you may want to "clean house" every so often and remove any outdated, irrelevant information. You can put what you'll never need again in the office recycling bin and archive the rest in a standard filing cabinet for future reference.

High-Tech Record Keeping

There are, of course, many computerized systems for tracking contacts available in the market. On the software side, they range from basic mailing list programs that can be customized to provide a few additional features—such as the ability to generate standard reports, sales letters, and contracts—to more complicated programs that will dial the phone for you or remind you what's on your calendar each day.

On the hardware end, there's everything from scanners that will scan your business cards into your computer (no typing!) to handheld "palmtop" computers that can be outfitted with electronic schedulers and portable fax machines to take on the road. Appendix F provides you with a few options.

But even if you outfit yourself with the latest technology, you may discover something like our "low-tech" binder is a necessity, if only as a backup. How many times have you been on the telephone with someone, only to hear them say, "Just a moment, the computer is acting up again," or "This computer is really slow today," or, simply, "My computer is broken and out for repair"? Any computer program should allow you to print out a general information sheet on each client and any important proposal, so you can insert this vital paperwork in your alphabetized folder as a backup.

As a customer, one experience that has given me the greatest number of laughs—or tears, depending on my mood—involves a "high-tech" computer store, the only one within a reasonable driving range that carried the brand of supplies I need. Although I've done a fair amount of business with this store, I can never rely on their sales staff to tell me where we left off. Everything is comput-

HARD WORK CAN MAKE LIFE EASIER

Ironically, what salespeople who like to "make life easy" don't realize, is: *What looks like the easy way out in the beginning is often the most difficult road to follow in the end.*

A young friend, who is highly intelligent if not brilliant, felt that high school was too much of a bother. Under pressure from his parents, he finally graduated—barely. College was out of the question. He certainly wasn't going to put forth the effort and put up with all of the bother it would take to earn a college degree. So, following high school he spent months at sea working on fishing boats in bitter weather or as a busboy and waiter. He lived with roommates and gave up his car in order to support himself. His jobs were unstable. When asked if he enjoyed them, he said no. His "easy way out" resulted in a hard life, indeed! Happily, he finally realized that sticking to something and "paying his dues" in an industry would lead to fewer personal hardships.

I contrast his experience with that of another friend. For eight years, she spent many sleepless nights and long hours as a medical student and resident. No one could say that experience wasn't exhausting and at times unpleasant. But she now earns over $100,000 a year, working only three days a week. The rest of the time she spends enjoying family life in her house on eleven acres, complete with a stable for the pony and a swimming pool.

But how does this apply to sales, you may ask? A salesman I once knew balked at filing call reports, analyzing his sales activities, or setting daily and weekly sales goals. Finally, the deadline for his project arrived, as did the day of reckoning. He was shocked to discover that, while he thought he had been doing okay, he was actually 30 percent under the revenue that the territory had brought in just six months before. He scrambled to make up the deficit at the last minute, but was unable to do so. Needless to say, the company let him go soon after. He had made things easy for himself all right—easy for him to lose his job!

The bottom line is that good records are essential to any successful sales effort. They help you keep track of your priorities, your clients, and your sales effort. Good records help you serve clients better and, at the very least, convey the message to prospects that they are highly valued business partners. In many ways that we haven't explained yet, but will get to in future chapters, with a good record-keeping system, you'll always know where you stand, how you are spending your time, what works, and what doesn't. A record-keeping system is a tool that will prove indispensable, slanting the odds in favor of your succeeding at sales.

Exercise: Decorate your workspace with pictures of benefits, rewards, and other positive reasons you want to succeed at sales.

erized—organized by number! If I call and say, "I ordered this cable for my computer about a month ago, and I want another just like it," they won't have a clue how to help me unless I also have the invoice number. If I've lost or filed my invoice, that's just too bad! And, even if I have my merchandise pickup slip, that isn't necessarily a help. The invoice number usually isn't printed on it anyway.

All of this makes me feel like a number, not a human being. It certainly doesn't build my loyalty as a customer. In fact, when I can spare the time, I often make the hour drive to another store that offers the same product!

Another fact to consider when relying on technology to help you in your sales efforts is the learning curve you'll have to endure before you can use the stuff. I remember well how excited I was when I purchased a sophisticated accounting program that was supposed to help me generate invoices, expense reports, financial statements, and more. A week later I still didn't know how to use the darn thing, even though I'd been happily operating a computer for two decades. Moreover, I didn't have the time to learn how to use it! I returned the fancy program and made do with my old one.

Each time you opt for a new piece of technology—whether hardware (a machine, like a computer) or software (a computer program)—you need to build in time to learn how to use it. Using a "low-tech" record keeper will prevent your sales effort from stalling while you're becoming a computer whiz.

As we've seen, having the best technology isn't a guarantee of efficiency, customer satisfaction, or success. You still have to arrange things so the information you need is readily accessible!

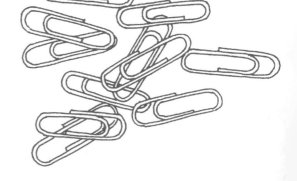

Combating Fear and Laziness in the Sales Office

Keeping good records is essential, yet many salespeople hate doing it. Why?

- They don't enjoy writing, anything, at any time, period.
- They view keeping records as too time-consuming, and think their time is better spent speaking to contacts or being in front of prospects.
- They think writing down information about sales calls and contacts is too bothersome; selling is difficult enough.

These are some of the most common excuses sales managers hear when they ask salespeople where the report on sales activities is that they were supposed to hand in weeks ago.

It's true that the salesperson who never "gets in front" of prospects, whether by telephone or in person, will fail. But no one is asking you to *never* call or visit clients and prospects. And you are not expected to write a book on each and every phone call. The key here—as in so much of sales—is balance.

Another reason salespeople do not like to keep records, and one they rarely admit, is fear. They are afraid that if they keep track of what they're doing, they'll have to look at what they're doing. What if they aren't doing enough? What if they are off track? *What if it looks as if they're not going to meet their sales goal?*

All human beings experience fear or discomfort when they tackle a new project or when they tackle a project in which they have a lot invested. Even though fear is a common emotion, it isn't a very useful one if your response is to bury your head in the sand.

Doesn't it make sense to keep tabs on your progress, so you aren't surprised later on? By checking on a day-to-day and week-to-week basis, you can track your progress and figure out how to rechart your path to bring you closer to meeting your goal.

CHAPTER 9

Getting an Appointment

You've got your lead list together and you've started to make calls. You've begun the precall-planning process on some potential clients. You've actually filled out a handful of customer information sheets. At this point, you have probably identified some prospects that you'd like to pursue further. Remember, they are worth pursuing for the following reasons:

- They have needs that aren't being filled.
- They have money to pay someone to help them fulfill those needs.
- You have the ability to fulfill those needs.
- The timing is right for you to pursue the sale.

Now you need to follow up with an in-person sales call. But before you actually meet with the client, you need to get an appointment.

Getting an appointment with a prospect is critical. An old maxim among salespeople is that "no one buys from a company, they buy from a person." One could argue this point: A company's size and reputation often do make a sale, but all too often inferior products and services sell over superior ones because the buyer feels better connected to the salesperson. There are many more opportunities for the buyer to bond with you during a face-to-face meeting, and many more opportunities for you to gauge their interest and needs. So, whenever possible, meet the client in person.

Sometimes, just working your way through the precall-planning process will spur the prospect into suggesting that the two of you meet. But more often then not, you'll be the one to ask the prospect for a meeting.

If you've been following the process outlined in earlier chapters, you'll be ideally positioned to ask for an appointment. You've already explained to the decisionmaker that your intention was to gather some information about her needs (or the needs of the company), and it's only natural to follow up that information-gathering process by asking her if she'd be interested in meeting to take the discussion further. Essentially, you just need to let the decisionmaker know that you'd like to help her if you could.

Here are some suggestions you might follow in asking for an appointment.

- "Mr. Decisionmaker, I hear you telling me that you need [the prospect's ideal situation] to happen. It doesn't sound as though your current [solution] is giving you quite the results you'd like. I'd like to take some time to think about your [need or problem] and then meet with you to brainstorm some options."

- "Now that I know a little more about your [problem] and your [need], Ms. Smith, I'd like to see if I can come up with a better solution. There are some [products or services] my company offers that might interest you. Could we meet in a couple of weeks to discuss some possible alternatives?"

- "I'm really interested in what you're saying about [the problem], Mr. Walker. It sounds as though you'd like to see [the prospect's ideal situation] happen. If I can think of some options for [achieving better results], would you be interested in hearing them?

- "It sounds as if you're pretty satisfied with the [current solution to the problem]. I'd still like to meet with you, Ms. Jones, just to review what my company can offer. Before you make your decision to buy from [Company X], I'd like the opportunity to show you what I can do for you."

- "If I could show you how to address [the problem], would you be interested in hearing some of my solutions?"

- "I hear you saying that you'd like to achieve [the prospect's ideal scenario], Ms. Richards. My company is in the business of helping companies such as yours [solve the problem]. Does it make sense for us to get together?"

- "Even though you're not in the market for [whatever you sell that will address the need] at this time, I'd like to meet with you. I'm new to the field, Mr. Brown, and I would appreciate hearing what you have to say about [problems facing in the industry]. Even if I can't provide you with a solution at the moment, by finding out more about what you need, I might be able to come up with a better solution when [the contract comes up for renewal]. "

- "Ms. Adams, I can't really say what we might be able to offer you [over the telephone] at this time. I need to talk to some people in my company and review some of the [new products or services] we're coming out with that I think might interest you. May we set an appointment to discuss the options?"

- "Your problem sounds very challenging, Mr. Collins. You need [summarize the prospect's problem and needs; briefly state each need]. It sounds as though you need a custom solution. I'd like to see if there's any way I can help you. May I put something together and meet with you in two weeks?"

- "My company is new to the [area or industry], Ms. Rogers. I understand your company is involved in [company goals]. I'd like to get together with you to learn more about what you do."

- "Mr. Widget, I'm your new sales rep for [your company name]. We've never met, and I'd like to get together to learn a bit more about your business and see whether I can help you in any way."

Practice Being Rejected

Asking the prospect for a meeting can be scary if you've never done it before. What if the prospect says no? You'll have to deal with rejection! That's why some novice salespeople don't even ask for an appointment. They think hinting is the same as asking. It's not. Don't be afraid to ask for an appointment. (In Chapter 12, I'll tell you the same thing about asking for the sale.)

If the prospect refuses to meet with you, don't worry. In the beginning, before you've had a lot of practice, you may not be successful getting a lot of appointments. In fact, some sales trainers suggest calling on candidates who aren't as critical to the success of your sales campaign to gain experience before tackling those you regard as most likely to need your services. In Chapter 16, we'll talk about how to evaluate your prospecting results and improve the picture. But for now the best thing you can do is simply gain some experience and practice your technique.

There are many ways to word a request for an appointment, but successful approaches essentially all do the same things:

- Focus on the customer's needs, summarizing, where possible, the customer's problems
- Hold out the promise of a solution (or, if the problem is "solved" for the moment, a better solution)
- Position the salesperson as a "consultant" who will "research" a solution taking the prospect's needs into account
- Imply that the buyer and seller are "partners" brainstorming ideas together
- Require an investment, if only psychological, by the buyer, by making a point of asking the buyer if a meeting would be "helpful" and leaving it up to the buyer to decide whether a meeting is appropriate
- Prevent the seller from "spilling his or her guts" and giving away every last piece of information on the phone before a meeting ever takes place

and, last but not least, they

- Ask for a meeting—at a time that allows for sufficient research but is not so distant that the prospect forgets who the salesperson is and why he or she called

Communication Tips

One aspect of asking for an appointment that won't be apparent to you from reading the dialogue box is the way you *say* the words. It's important to speak at a lively pace. Most people don't have a lot of time these days, so you don't want to drag things out and try their patience. Make sure that the tone you use when

asking the questions is soothing and conversational. Try to be expressive, or you won't capture the listener's attention. Express sincere concern about their problems and an eagerness to work with the client on resolving them.

What If a Prospect Refuses to Meet with You?

Sometimes a prospect's refusal to meet is an almost automatic response, a way for them to avoid acknowledging that they might have a problem to fix or a need to address. You may have skipped some essential questions in the precall planning stage, or not listened carefully enough to their responses. Try going through the questioning process again. Keep in mind that at this stage you are:

1. Asking questions
2. Listening to the customer's response
3. *Not* giving out information about what you do (because you can't really help the prospect until you have more information about what they do)

If prospects seem worried that you're going to put them through a "high-pressure" sales pitch, assure them that just the opposite is true. One seasoned sales rep I worked with used to tell her clients, "I take a no as graciously as I take a yes."

Although you should never put the customer on the defensive, sometimes it's okay to be blunt and strong, especially with entrepreneurial types. Here are a couple of examples of what I mean:

- "Don't you owe it to yourself to be fully informed about all of the options before you make a decision?"
- "Mr. Decisionmaker, I don't work on commission. I'm not trying to get you to buy something you don't want. I'm only trying to get you to thoroughly evaluate my product or service and consider how it might add value for you."

CHECKLIST

Home Your Selling Skills

Here are a few more ways you can get some selling experience:

❑ Write a list of possible objections and good ways to counter them (Keep the list posted above your desk so you can review them until they become "second nature.")

❑ Ask a prospect who says no for help (What would make them change their mind? Is there any way you can improve what you have to offer or your sales technique?)

❑ Take advantage of opportunities to practice "selling" whenever you can in everyday life (Use casual conversation with friends and strangers to sell a positive outlook, charitable donations, a proposal for the school board, chores to your children, and so forth.)

❑ Practice introducing yourself to strangers and asking them questions ("Why are you buying that mop?" "Are you an avid gardener? What plants do you favor? Why?")

Keeping the Door Open

Leave the door open even if you don't get the appointment on this phone call. For example, you can say:

- "Tom, I hear what you are saying. Tell you what, I'll just send you the literature anyway and give you a chance to take a look at it." (Here's an opportunity to use some of that neat stuff you put together for your sales tool kit!)

- "Thanks for talking with me today, Cindy. I'll give you a chance to reflect on this solution further. Then I'll call you next time I'm in this area."

- "Thanks for your time today. May I keep in touch, Mr. Jones, just to see how things are going?"

- "I'll give you a call in a few months, Ms. Smith, when our new products come out."

If the customer sounds preoccupied, you may want to ask if there is a better time for you to call. If he is thinking about something else, you probably aren't going to be able to get very far—not now, anyway. Or maybe the customer just wants you to know that she really isn't feeling particularly receptive to your call. At least by asking her if there is a better time to call, you are acknowledging that you understand she is sounding less than positive and that you are thinking of her perspective, not just yours.

The prospect may have a valid reason for refusing to see you. Moving the office, switching jobs, or a long-term contract with another company are all plausible reasons for not making an appointment just yet. Nevertheless, you are not without some options here: You can ask them when to call back. Then send them a postcard thanking them for their time and mentioning that you will call back at the time indicated. Just be sure to call them back at the suggested time (instead of writing them off).

Being gracious when the prospect refuses you lets the prospect know that you do indeed take no graciously. Because you responded to his or her no with warmth and cheerfulness, the prospect will probably agree to talk to you again when you call later. They won't fear a high-pressure pitch or some other hassle.

Most likely you will get a no from many clients before you ever get a yes. Working through the noes over time by accepting them graciously and continuing to keep in touch with the client will often convert a no to a yes.

Remember, if you called to set up an appointment, stay with that objective. Don't try to close the sale. As soon as your prospects show enough interest so you think they will agree to see you in person, go for it—set up the appointment. Don't risk the appointment by trying to sell. Save additional talk for the in-person visit.

COLD CALL FOR HOT LEADS

Another way to meet decisionmakers is to drop in on them at their workplace without notice. This is known in sales lingo as a *cold call*, presumably because you have had no prior contact, you didn't even know that the prospect existed until you saw their office in the same building as one of your other clients, or they have already refused to meet with you—and therefore, as far as you know, they aren't even a warm lead.

Cold calling consists of dropping in at the prospect's office during normal business hours. Dressed in business attire, you walk in and ask if the individual is available and can he step out of his office to meet you for a minute. You can explain that you merely want to say hello, introduce yourself, or drop off some literature or other material that might interest him. If the prospect is available, shake hands, explain with a smile that you were in the neighborhood and thought you'd stop in to say hello and introduce yourself, deliver the material, whatever. The idea is to make it clear this is a brief, casual visit. It is not intended to take up the prospect's time but rather to allow both you and the client to put a "face" to a name and make personal contact.

As a novice salesperson you may be unwilling to drop in on a client unexpectedly, fearing that it will annoy, interrupt, or disturb the client. Don't be. If a prospect is in a meeting or is too busy to see you, she'll let you know, and you can leave the information or tell the receptionist you'll stop back another day. Many people fear cold calls, because prospects can sometimes be short or express disinterest. But the benefits of a cold call invariably outweigh the negatives. In today's increasingly impersonal business world, even a busy prospect will be impressed that you took the time to say hello in person. And many times you'll find people are more pleasant in person than on the telephone. Often, if you catch a prospect during a lull, you'll get the opportunity to gather information in person.

At the very least, by visiting the prospect's workplace, you'll have a bit more information than you previously had to use in a phone call and something to break the ice when you get the prospect on the phone. And don't forget to follow up with a note; it gives you an extra opportunity to bond with the prospect (see Appendix B for a sample cold-call follow-up note).

CHAPTER 10

Three Steps to Prepare for a Sales Meeting

A typical sales meeting consists of the following steps:

- Introducing yourself to the client
- Getting an overall sense of the client's situation
- Asking strategic questions to identify the client's needs and what he or she wants to do about satisfying them
- Presenting your products or service solutions tailored to the customer's needs
- Overcoming objections
- Asking for the sale
- Drawing up a contract
- Following up on the sales call

Short and simple though this agenda is, it is easy to lose focus in a sales meeting, especially if you are new to selling. A good salesperson must stay focused, be aware of his or her agenda at all times, and learn to "read" the client while allowing things to appear to develop naturally. Selling is a bit like a skill or an art—thankfully, it's one anyone can learn! In the next two chapters, we'll walk you step-by-step through a sales meeting.

But before we get to the actual appointment, I want to give you a few tips on preparing for a client meeting. Since you are a salesperson and business consultant, it is up to you to do your best to make the call a success.

Step 1: Plan to Keep Control of the Sales Process

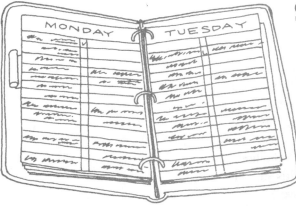

Planning the call before it happens is critical. But since we've already talked about that in Chapter 6 on precall planning, I won't repeat those steps again, except to say, study your customer information sheet and review any other information you have regarding the company's needs. Familiarize yourself with what you know about the key people involved in the decision-making process and the process itself.

Write down the important needs, concerns, and other issues that you need to raise at the meeting. List the questions you need to ask the customer (we'll talk more about that in Chapter 11). Outline some possible solutions from your end.

Step 2: Dress the Part

One of the first things the customer is going to notice is your dress and grooming. It's important to make some general points about dressing to succeed at sales now, while you're preparing for a client meeting.

Many articles have been written about what to wear to work. During the 1980s and early 1990s, a lot of salespeople were told to spend money on expensive business suits and status accessories (e.g., a Rolex watch) to look as successful as possible, or to don the Ivy League uniform—a Brooks Brothers suit with a discreetly striped ("rep") or dotted tie.

Over the last ten years, however, clothing rules for the workplace have become more and more relaxed. For example, I know of one team at a Fortune 500 corporation that was working on developing a major proposal for a customer about a year ago. There would be no question in my mind that any consultant would advise this team to dress in gray suits with white shirts and ties, and the conservative equivalent for the women. In fact, this corporation requires all employees to dress in this fashion. However, the customer actually requested that the salespeople dress casually for all meetings with them!

I remember a sales team in the designer-conscious eighties that consisted of two people who represented an upscale magazine. The "schlepper" (the company nickname for the salesperson who was casually dressed, had somewhat untidy hair, and always toted a soft-sided briefcase overflowing with papers) consistently sold more than the saleswoman with the neat suit and polished bob. Since then I've seen many more salespeople performing successfully in the business world dressed far more casually than I expected.

The truth is, there are no hard-and-fast rules for business attire. Looking clean, neat, and organized definitely slants the odds in your favor, but beyond that, you need to do a bit of detective work.

KEY IDEAS

Plan for Success

Success will come your way if you keep your focus and manage your time well by outlining an agenda for the meeting and bringing it with you to your appointment.

Don't Dress to Divert

Many new sales reps get caught up in buying clothes and forget their goal—to partner with their client. The focus should be on the customer, not on you. Remember that your intent is to link your product or service features with the customer's needs or problems. Never dress to detract or distract from your product or service. The more you divert the customer's attention from the solution being offered, the fewer your chances of developing that critical linkage between your potential client and your product or service. You must realize that for your customers, as well as for yourself, time is money. They want to get right down to business. Rather than making what you wear the center of attention, you want the answers your product or service provides to take center stage. You want to keep building their confidence in your abilities by sending them the quiet signals that will make them both comfortable and confident in their choice of you as a vendor.

Consider the image you are trying to project to the customer. Relate your dress to your customer's level of dress. What is your customer's and your industry's unwritten dress code? Is an inexpensive folkloric dress made of cheap, imported rayon the appropriate attire to sell a $100,000 diamond ring to a client in a discreet upscale jewelry store located in the heart of the posh downtown shopping district? In America's culture, no. A conservative navy blue suit assures the buyer that she is handing over large sums of money to someone who is trustworthy. Is Farmer John going to be impressed with a $2,000 custom-tailored Italian suit? You might be better off wearing a plaid shirt to sell that tractor. Are you in the fashion industry? Then you'll need to show some style.

On the other hand, don't overdo the casual bit. It's true that wearing a business suit to call on someone in construction gives the impression you don't like to get your hands dirty and might not know what you're talking about when it comes to the business trades. Dressing in khakis and a nice casual shirt with a collar helps the prospect identify with you and presents a more competent impression than worn jeans and a T-shirt.

Once again, using the construction sales example, think about how the potential customer would react if the salesperson arrived in expensive designer khakis, with an obviously costly designer shirt and imported shoes. Can you imagine how hard it would be for the field foreman to listen to the sales presentation when he's wondering, "Where the heck did you get that outfit?" and "How are you ever going to get out on the site?"

What you are carrying can send an important message, too. It is better to carry too little than too much to a first meeting. Remember, you are still trying to learn about your customer's business. On an initial visit be wary of carrying an inappropriately large number of sample boxes. Too many sample boxes may make a buyer feel uneasy. She might think you have unrealistically high expectations for the first meeting. The buyer also may feel that she is being pressured into having a longer or more serious meeting than was planned.

Don't forget the small details such as shoes, handbags, belts, and briefcases. Make sure they are in good shape and not overly worn! Your accessories should convey the same appropriate style as the other attire you select.

Step 3: Time Your Arrival

Be exactly five minutes early. No more, no less. Being late is an easy way to tell buyers you don't respect them and don't value their time. Rushing to a sales appointment is a sure way to arrive frazzled, something the buyer is likely to pick up on; thus it risks endangering the tone of the meeting.

Being early is better than being late . . . but it still could cause you to lose the sale. Arriving too early may tell the customer that you are either nervous or overeager (desperate). Even if you feel calm, the buyer will be less relaxed thinking that you might be nervous. And if the buyer is less relaxed, it will be more difficult to build rapport and gain trust.

Another problem with being more than five minutes early is that the customer may feel pressured to see you before the appointed time. You may be thinking that you are in no rush to see the buyer; maybe it is your only appointment of the day. But your physical presence sends another message: "I am here . . . I am doing nothing else . . . I am available to see you now." Some buyers won't feel pressured by your being extra early, but some will. At the typical business office, the receptionist will almost always call the prospect right when you arrive. If you are calling on someone in an office or a home where there is no receptionist, the customer may feel even more pressured and more off balance by your unexpected early presence.

Being relaxed when you meet the customer is important, and it is not just a matter of luck. Always have something with you to read, so you won't fidget and get edgy before your meeting. A copy of a magazine, newspaper, or newsletter relating to the industry would be good. If the prospect catches you reading appropriate literature, it will show him that you manage your time well—and suggest that you won't waste his. It will also tell him that you are keeping abreast of news that's important to his industry. In some cases, if there's an article that relates to the customer's situation, it can even serve as an icebreaker.

You can also use this time to observe your surroundings to see if they can provide clues to your client's interest, needs, or business. Perhaps something in the office will provide an icebreaker later on.

Be Five Minutes Early

How can you be exactly five minutes early every time?

Allow enough time so that even if traffic is heavier than expected, you will still arrive early. Then go to a coffee shop in the immediate neighborhood or wait in your car in the parking lot. Make a couple of phone calls if you want. Then time your arrival for exactly five minutes before the scheduled appointment time.

CHAPTER 11

Anatomy of a Sales Call, Part I:
From Meeting and Greeting to the Sales Presentation

Meet and Greet with Confidence

There is a right way and a wrong way to shake hands. You want to reach out with your right hand and give a very firm handshake (not a vise grip). Don't wait for the buyer to extend his or her hand. Take the initiative, if the customer doesn't. Even if your customer offered a weak handshake, by extending your hand within a second or two of the customer's approach, you make a personal connection and convey respect at the same time.

● ● ●

Don't Waste Time in Too Much Small Talk

Remember how much time you have for the appointment, and be sure to get down to business in plenty of time. Otherwise you could find yourself talking to a prospect for half an hour about irrelevant things and discover the prospect has to leave before you cover your agenda. It doesn't hurt to ask the prospect up-front, "How much time do we have?"

The first few minutes of your meeting are crucial. Like building a house on a cracked foundation, it's a lot more difficult to build a positive sales relationship, if you don't start out on the "right foot." In the initial moments of the meeting, impressions will be formed quickly, a tone will develop, chemistry will or won't develop, and the foundation for the rest of your interactions with the customer will be built. We all form almost instantaneous subjective judgments about people we meet; once they are formed, they are hard to change. This is bad news if your first impression is weak. But it's great news if your first impression is strong.

The Greeting

Making a great first impression varies from culture to culture. Books have been written about how the Japanese do business, how the Arabs do business, and so forth. We won't cover international sales here! But we will talk about what you need to do to form a great first impression in the good old United States.

Project a positive and confident attitude right from the start. Stand up straight, look the prospect in the eye, and smile warmly. Standing about an arm's length from the client, extend your hand for a handshake.

Looking the customer in the eye is important. If you look away, you'll distance yourself. People think that if you can't look them in the eyes, you are untrustworthy (remember that old adjective *shifty-eyed*?).

Even in our super-casual society, a handshake is still the expected method of greeting someone. As soon as the customer is within reach, just as you are beginning to shake hands, you should introduce yourself. Again, you don't have to wait for the customer to take the initiative. Chances are the customer's mind is probably still focused on the last appointment or issue she was facing. Help bring the customer to focus on how you can help with a strong, confident address, such as: "Jane Decisionmaker, I assume. I'm [your name]." (Simultaneous handshake.) "It's a pleasure to meet you!" (Genuine warmth in voice and good eye contact.)

If the customer steps slightly forward or back, stay where you are. The customer is moving to the distance at which she feels most comfortable.

Alternatively, the customer might sit down and politely beckon you to do the same. If the customer sits and doesn't beckon, you should just take an available seat anyway—don't make the situation awkward by asking "May I have a seat?" Be sure not to sit down until after the customer does. This may sound like a small detail, but sitting down even a few seconds before the customer is discourteous and will offend some people.

Breaking the Ice

After sharing introductions, you will almost always want to engage in some small talk. Why is this so important? Small talk helps build rapport and a pleasant, nonconfrontational conversational bond. Good small talk can help set the tone for discussing substantive issues; no small talk leaves you without a foundation for beginning your presentation. Building a strong bond early is particularly important when you want to be able to get the customer comfortably talking to you about his business issues as soon as possible, rather than just passively listening to you make your sales pitch.

Ideally you want to roll smoothly right from the introductions into small talk. Try to avoid awkward silences. Almost in the same breath that you introduce yourself, start a two-way conversation. Often you will want to begin simply with "How is your day going?" This kind of question is polite, it is not obtrusive, and it will often get the customer talking. It shows that you are focused on the customer. And it also leaves the ball in the customer's court—giving him the chance to open up in conversation, or to signal to you, with a curt answer, that he wants to get to business quickly.

Here are some other ways to break the ice:

- *Refer to common interests*. Is it possible for you to begin the conversation with a positive reference to a mutual acquaintance—perhaps the person who referred you to this customer? Do you belong to any of the same clubs or associations? Did you attend the same or similar schools?

Icebreakers

Here are a few examples.

- "I'm really impressed with your product line, Mr. Boss. Are you adding many new items next year?"
- "I've personally used your firm's services, Ms. Smith, and I was very impressed by them. Do you serve the entire metro area now?"
- "This is a beautiful home, John. Have you been here long?"
- "I was just in your new format store last week, Ms. Designer, and I was surprised to see how much larger it seemed. Are you going to convert many existing stores to the new layout?"
- "I just read about the big 17 percent sales increase over the past year, Mr. Buyer. Do you think you'll be able to keep up such fast growth this year?"

Transitioning to Sales

Here are a few suggestions for accomplishing the transition from small talk to sales.

- "Well, Bob, I'm glad we had an opportunity to sit down today. I would love to explore if we might be able to help you better serve the needs of your customers, or help you lower costs or achieve other efficiencies [i.e., summarize whatever the problem/issue/need he previously expressed to you]."

- "Linda, thanks for meeting with me. I'd like to find out what your main concerns are in using services such as ours. Then I'd like to see if we can offer you any true advantages in these areas."

- "Jim, to be helpful to you, I'd like to hear a little bit about your business and your customers. Then we can talk about what [your company] does and what our next step might be."

- "Since we haven't met before, Ms. Smith, you may not know much about [your company]. We know that everybody's business is a little different, so we have specialized in custom work for the past fifteen years. We like to use this first meeting to understand more about what you do so we can tailor our recommendations to those needs."

Don't fabricate or overplay a common interest, but if it's there, see if you can work it into the conversation.

You don't have to have been a fraternity brother or sorority sister to have common interests with a prospective customer. There are many other areas in which you may have common interests with your prospective customer. If you both work in the same industry, you could ask, "Are you ready for the trade show next week?" If the customer lives in the same town, you could ask, "Did you see the big parade last weekend?"

- *Show an interest in or admiration for the customer.* A positive comment about the customer helps set a good positive tone, but don't overdo it by being insincere. Ask a question or make a statement that may get the customer talking in a positive way, rather than simply saying, "Thank you."

- *Pick up cues from the office.* Sure, it's a very traditional approach to start the conversation with a comment about something in your client's office, but it can be a good approach! Those items wouldn't be displayed if he or she didn't enjoy talking about the subject. The key is not to be phony. Don't say, "Oh, I love fishing!" if you've never gone fishing. Instead you could say, "Oh, you're a fisherman. I've never tried it, but I'd like to. What do you suggest for a beginner?" Again, you are coming from a foundation of honesty and truth. People will appreciate that. Make a comment or two, but keep it short unless the customer keeps the conversation going.

Making the Transition to Sales

Generally you will want to keep your small talk or comments to a short sentence or two. If the buyer appears genuinely interested in developing the conversation further, go with the flow for a while. But remember how much time you have in the appointment, and be sure to save plenty of time for business. Once you feel the small talk is beginning to slow down at all (listen for fading voice tone and slower rate of speech), switch into business right away.

CUSTOMERS DON'T WANT TO BE SOLD; CUSTOMERS WANT TO BUY

I'm sure you've come across the image of the used-car salesman, our culture's way of making fun of pushy and aggressive "salesmen." If you are a beginner at sales, you may even be questioning your ability to sell because you don't see yourself—and you don't want to see yourself—as a "pushy salesperson." Well, you needn't worry. Pushy salespeople are seldom successful in the long run. Most sales trainers I've met agree on at least one thing: No customer wants to be "sold." Selling is not about convincing someone they need what you have. It's not about browbeating someone into buying what you have to sell. Selling is about identifying who needs what you have and being the one to get it for them.

Customers don't want to be sold; customers want to buy. That is, they want to feel that they have decided, without being pushed, to buy a product or service because it fulfills a need that they have.

In other words, selling is about enabling customers to sell themselves. The customer is the true salesperson! You are only a facilitator helping customers identify the best solutions for themselves or their business.

Try practicing these affirmations:

- *I am looking for people who need what I have.*
- *Customers want to buy.*
- *I am fulfilling the prospect's needs.*
- *My customers sell themselves.*
- *I am helping my clients identify the best solutions for themselves and their businesses.*

CHECKLIST

Four Essential Questions to Answer in Openers

❑ Who are you?
❑ What is your company all about?
❑ How long is this going to take?
❑ What am I doing here?

●●●

Why Ask Questions?

❑ To discover why the prospect agreed to meet with you
❑ To find out what goals and objectives the customer has
❑ To find out what motivates the customer
❑ To find out what strategies or tactics he or she hopes to use to achieve his or her objectives
❑ To find out what issues trigger the customer's concern or interest
❑ To find out what the customer's "hot buttons" are
❑ To find out the customer's decision-making process

- *Listen.* A big part of being a successful salesperson is listening— to what the customer says, to what the customer does not say, and to body language. Even while sharing greetings, you may very quickly get the message that this person does not want to engage in any small talk. Maybe the customer will be curt with you. For example, when you ask, "How are you today?" she may abruptly answer, "Fine." Or maybe she will make it clear to you with body language that she is in a rush. Or maybe she will be verbally explicit by saying something like, "So, what have you got for me?"

- *Be responsive.* If the customer is signaling to you that he or she doesn't want to engage in small talk, don't force it! Take the cue and get right down to business. This will show customers that you appreciate their feelings, you are listening to them, and you understand that your job is to be responsive to their needs.

- *Outline an agenda.* One of the best ways to switch to business and to start emphasizing the focus on the customer is to give a summary of what you hope to accomplish during the meeting—to outline an agenda. If you have followed the suggestions in Chapter 10 on preparing for a sales meeting, you will already have prepared an agenda by this point, and it should be easy for you to present it to the prospect.

  Start with a transition such as thanking the person for getting together with you today. You want to emphasize in a sincere way that you are here to help the customer achieve his or her goals—not just to sell your products or services. Right from the start, you want to make it clear that you are not here to waste time or just try to meet your sales quota; you are here to help the customer find solutions.

  For more complex selling situations, you may want to give a copy of the agenda to the customer when you begin the sales call. While you are summarizing your agenda at the beginning of the meeting, ask the customer, "While I'm here, is there anything else you'd like to accomplish?" Let them add to the agenda before you start. This gets the customer right on board by sharing ownership of the agenda. It lets the customer know that his or her concerns are an integral part of the meeting. Setting an agenda tells the customer that your meeting will have direction and purpose and underscores the need for you to ask "all those questions."

Also try to get a sense of how much time you have for the meeting, so you can plan your agenda accordingly. If possible, establish the amount of time the prospect can spend with you before you arrive. If you forgot to do that, you might ask, "How much time do we have?" Generally, I've found that a good meeting—one that explores the prospect's needs rather thoroughly—takes a half hour to an hour. Depending on the complexity of the item you're selling, yours may be shorter or longer.

Building Trust by Asking Questions

Trust is more than just convincing buyers that you are honest, although this certainly is essential. You must also convince them that they are not going to waste their time or money by dealing with you. Every buyer has been burned by salespeople in one way or another. You can easily lose the buyer's trust in a second. You need to work very hard to win that trust, and sometimes it might take a while for it to develop.

Trust is the foundation of every good sale. Trust means that the prospective customers believe in you. They must respect your product knowledge, your service standards, your sales abilities, and your approach to the business. In essence, they like you, they like how you operate, and they trust you.

If you've followed the steps outlined thus far, you have already effectively set the tone in the beginning of your sales call by acknowledging the other person, setting an agenda, and giving an overview of yourself and your company. By covering these bases, you have answered the prospect's initial questions about you: Who are you? What is this company all about? How long is this going to take? What am I doing here? By setting the tone up-front, you reduce the prospect's concerns, appear organized and concise, and lay the groundwork for additional trust building.

KEY IDEAS

Three Steps to Build Trust

Building trust with your client during a sales call is a three-step process.

1. Search in depth for the specifics of the customer's particular needs.
2. Explore solutions with customers and gain agreement on what your product or service needs to do for them.
3. Explain how your product will produce the desired solution.

•••

Selling Requires More Listening than Talking

Communication—and good selling—requires more listening than talking. When you're quiet, it encourages prospects to talk. Give them a chance to respond!

KEY IDEAS

Dialogues Build Trust

You'll get further by asking questions than by making statements. Asking questions builds a two-way dialogue.

- Dialogues build trust.
- Dialogues help you find out what the buyer wants.
- Dialogues help make the buyer more comfortable with you.
- Dialogues discourage you from making long-winded pitches about how great your product is.

Customers need to be able to trust that you are there to help them find a solution first—not just to push products or services. The trouble is, customers are predisposed to assume that you, like many other salespeople, want to sell as much product as fast as you can, at as high a price as you can, and then rush along to the next account. Throughout the entire sales process, from the first phone call to agreement and follow-up, remember that customers may constantly be watching for any signs that you are just trying to dump products or services on them that don't meet their needs.

As the call progresses, prospects take in all the cues; they listen to your tone, and they watch your body language. To build trust, stay calm, be centered, be fully present, and focus your energy on the prospect. Concentrate on finding common ground. Leave your ego at the door, and always begin your sales meeting focused on the prospective client. Build rapport by letting the prospect talk.

Too many salespeople try to emphasize, right off the bat, a particular product feature or service. This approach may show that the product or service may help the customer, but it doesn't show that the salesperson can help the customer. It also makes the customer "protective" about talking to or meeting with the salesperson. He or she may be thinking, "Do I really have to talk with or meet with this salesperson? I just know that they are going to rant and rave about how great their product is and waste my time."

Remember: To build trust, do more listening than talking. Don't give into the pull of being a know-it-all. Restrain your ego, and keep in mind the following points:

- Forget about using canned pitches and elaborate sales aids to dazzle the customer!
- The customer does not want to be dazzled!
- The customer does not want to be sold your product!
- The customer does not care about your product!
- The customer cares about achieving his or her goals and creating his or her solutions!

Asking questions is not without risk. Asking the wrong questions can alienate the buyer or even end the sales meeting. This is why it is important to think out, in advance, the questions you want to ask—

TECHNIQUES FOR ASKING QUESTIONS

Here are a few techniques for asking questions.

1. *Layer questions.* Sometimes the first response you get from a customer may be too general or too standard. You may need to dig deeper (into another layer) and ask another question to elaborate upon the answer to the previous question.

> **Sales rep (selling marketing consulting service):** What is the vision for your marketing programs?
>
> **Decisionmaker:** Oh, well, our vision is to be the best in the industry. (Standard non-thinking answer.)
>
> **Sales rep:** Could you describe to me what that looks like to you?
>
> **Decisionmaker:** I guess specifically we want our name to be widely perceived as at least one of the top brands in the field in terms of market share and also in terms of quality. (Now this answer begins to give the sales rep more specific information.)

2. *Use closed-ended questions sparingly.* A closed-ended question generally elicits a simple answer such as yes or no. "What are your company's total yearly sales?" or "Do you have any plants overseas?"

    There are times when you need to get specific information and closed-ended questions are unavoidable, but since they are such conversation stoppers, you should try to follow-up a close-ended question with an open-ended question.

3. *Avoid choice questions.* Choice questions ("Do you use electric or oil heat?") are like closed-ended questions in that they elicit a short response and can stop the flow of the conversation. Use them sparingly as well.

4. *Move from general to specific.* Start with broader questions and narrow them down as you go along. Remember, you are heading in a direction—toward your goal for this client! Starting out with strictly product- or service-related questions—such as "How many do you use?" or "What kind do you usually order?" or "Who are you buying from now?"—makes it sound as if you are just interested in trying to figure out how much money you can make if you land the account! Instead, start from the broader perspective that is relevant to the decisionmaker you are meeting with.

5. *If all else fails, ask leading questions.* Sometimes you call on someone who's the human equivalent of a clam. Either they haven't given much thought to what they want to do, or they are afraid to let you know what they're thinking. Either way, it may behoove you to ask them questions that suggest problems or concerns to think about. The idea here is to jump-start their thinking process: "Mr. Decisionmaker, to be thorough, I'd like to ask you some general questions that most of my other clients in your industry are also concerned about. A key issue for many people in your situation is that the high cost of raw materials seems to be driving up manufacturing costs. Is that a problem for you?"

Sample Sales Questions

- "Ms. Smith, could you explain to me what some of your primary objectives are for this year?"

- "Could you describe to me for a minute, Mr. Brown, what you see the company looking like six months from now?"

- "Could you share with me your main concerns in this product area, Mr. Blank?"

- "Could you explain to me, Mary, how the service you are seeking ideally would meet your needs?"

- "Could you explore with me, Tom, how you envision an outside service interacting with your department?"

- "I remember you mentioned some problems that you were having in this area, Sue. Could you share with me any issues that particularly concern you?"

- "Could you share with me, Mr. Black, what characteristics you want most from your service provider?"

although you need to remain flexible and change the questions if the feedback from the customer dictates.

More often than not, though, the biggest risk in asking questions is that customers often assume you'll tell them information about your product, and when you reply to their questions with another question or put them off, they sometimes get irritated. Don't give in to this kind of discomfort! Asking prospects questions deflects attempts to garner information about your product and service before you have an understanding of their needs and can tailor a solution to satisfy them. It also confronts buyers with the fact that they have a need to solve that they might have been putting off solving.

No matter how insistent customers are, don't start explaining your product or service until you've explored their needs in detail. If they become insistent, "lay it on the line." Explain that you need to show that you are going to provide useful information, not just trumped-up sales points. Tell them that you need to show that it will be worthwhile to listen to you, not just because your product has a "feature" or a special price, but because you are going to help them by providing information they want. You need to show buyers that you are not going to cloud the delivery of information with a lot of "noise" or sales puffery about how great your product is or how much better it is than a competing product. And to do that, you need to know what their goals are and how you can help them.

You can explain to them that in today's world, product information is more plentiful than ever. There are product catalogs, product brochures, independent reviews, studies, and surveys. You can leave yours with the customer. But in your experience, today's customer has less and less need for general information about your product or service. They can usually get and refer to general information at their leisure. By asking questions, you can work with them to develop a customized solution to their needs, or at the very least a customized explanation of how your product or service can suit their needs. But you can't deliver this solution or deliver this explanation until you find out what their needs are.

To accurately assess the customer's situation, you'll need to ask at least several open-ended questions (i.e., questions that aren't answerable with yes or no). Good questions require preparation. The questions outlined in Chapter 6 on precall planning are a perfectly good place to start. Even if you've already asked the customer those questions, you now have the opportunity to verify what you already know. Sometimes in asking the same questions again, you'll find the prospect gives you a different answer altogether or more information than he or she did before. Asking questions that start with words such as *describe, explain, tell,* or *share* encourages the prospect to open up. Follow up with closed-ended questions that begin with words such as *do, does, is,* or *have* to zero in on specific information or confirm with the customer a summary of your understanding of his or her needs.

As you question, listen to what the customer is telling you. Good questions keep the customer involved in the sales process, and you may have to revise your preplanned questions accordingly. If your questions don't sound intelligent and stimulating or if the customer can't readily see that the questions might help find solutions, your sales call could be very short indeed. So make sure you give some good thought to what questions will sound good *and* help lead you to suggesting solutions for the customer. By asking strategic questions, you'll truly understand the prospect's needs and know exactly how to position your product or service as the best solution.

If you don't start asking questions, you may never know what your customer—or lost prospect—was really interested in. For example, if you emphasize service in your presentation, but your prospect is more interested in a certain feature, your prospect is not going to say, "I would have bought your product if you'd emphasized such and such feature." Instead, your prospect is going to buy from the salesperson who emphasizes that feature.

To summarize, you are trying to get inside the customer's mind to truly understand what is driving that person's thinking process and to get the information that will enable you to help him or her. You really need to create questions that will best fit not only your product or service but also each selling situation. The extra effort spent developing good ques-

KEY IDEAS

Shut Up and Sell

Even if the customer asks you for information, refrain from giving it to him or her at this time. Otherwise, you may discover the time available for meeting is spent on your giving the prospect all of your information without really concentrating on the prospect's needs. *Prospects often are so involved in asking and learning about your business, they even forget they have a need!* And if they don't have a need, you won't be selling them anything, because they won't need what you have to offer. So add some SASs to your meeting—shut up and sell!

•••

Shut Up and Sell Some More!

It may seem as though I'm covering a lot of stuff when I describe the information-gathering approach to a sales meeting, but here's the basic premise: *Don't give prospects any information about what you can do for them until you get their information!*

Don't Assume Anything

Don't make assumptions about the customer! Customers have different needs and concerns. Two very similar companies buying very similar products or services more often than not have some significantly different concerns or issues. This doesn't mean there isn't any similarity in their concerns—sure there is! But there are almost always enough differences that a canned presentation is going to miss their primary concerns. By asking questions, you don't have to leave to chance choosing the right features or products to emphasize; instead, you will know which to emphasize because you will have asked.

tions will go a long way in helping to find the best solution for your customers, to explain it to them, and ultimately to make the sale.

Reminder: Good questions should not stump the customer. Good questions should make the customer *think* about his or her problems and needs, and particularly about *the need for a solution.*

Very reserved buyers are going to give you information only because they perceive it will benefit them in some way. So the setup may need to be an explanation: "To be thorough," or "To best tell you how I may be able to help you, it would be helpful for me to know just a little more about what you do." Even most reserved buyers who are willing to meet with you will answer at least a few easy questions after a simple explanation like this one.

Keep in mind that some buyers need to process information for a while. Salespeople tend to talk a little faster and respond a little more quickly than most people. Some people need to think in order to come up with a careful answer to an investigative question. If you think this is the case, slow down and patiently wait for answers. Sometimes the customer will start with a very brief answer; if you don't jump in, and shut up for three pulses, that person may very well elaborate in a much more detailed response.

There is no cookie-cutter answer to how long you should spend asking questions. The more complicated or expensive the product or service, the more questions you'll need to ask to get the information you need to come up with a solution. The size of the potential sale may also impact how much depth and how many issues to investigate with a customer. For example, if you are selling courier services to a small business owner who requires only a couple of deliveries a week, you may want to spend a few minutes asking questions and exploring needs. On the other hand, you may want to spend a couple of hours exploring needs with the office manager of an international corporation that makes hundreds of courier shipments every day.

Acknowledging the Customer's Need

Too often in a sales situation the focus is on making your next point or quickly overcoming an objection. Instead, you need to really focus on and absorb what the customer is saying so you can think about helping the customer find a solution to his or her need. To help you focus, and

Software Consultant: You said you were getting lots of complaints. Are you losing money or customers because of poor service?

Decisionmaker: Probably. (Pause.) Yes.

Software Consultant: But are you losing enough customers to make it worthwhile looking into a solution?

Decisionmaker: How much do you charge?

Software Consultant: We offer a variety of packages, depending on your needs. I don't know how much money you could save through more efficiency. I wouldn't want to propose a solution that was too costly for you; the money you save should be relative to the money you spend. The goal here is to build your revenue by helping to service your clients better. Do you know what each lost call is costing you and the percentage of calls that are getting disconnected or that are unable to get through?

Decisionmaker: Oh, I couldn't say how many dollars I'm losing. I just know that for every three calls that come in, there are two that aren't being handled.

Software Consultant: Earlier you told me that your average sale was about $200. Maybe we can get a better sense of what's going on. (Takes out calculator.) Let's see, for every $1,000 worth of business, $400 represents dissatisfied customers. That's roughly 40 percent of your current customer base that you might have trouble getting to come back. Can you risk losing that much repeat business?

Decisionmaker: I'd really like to keep those customers coming back.

Software Consultant: Have you worked up a budget to overhaul your software?

Decisionmaker: Not really...But I can see that I need to spend some money on this.

Software Consultant (affirming the customer's decision)**:** I think you're making a smart decision. I'd like to work with you to establish some priorities and brainstorm a solution that's in the ballpark with regard to your budget.

to confirm your understanding of the situation, you need to acknowledge the customer's need.

Ideally with open-ended questions, customers will talk at length, telling you what's really on their mind. Often it won't be the specific information that will help you identify their need, but a follow-up comment the customer makes. Pay attention to this exchange:

Salesperson: Are there any paramount objectives or major challenges for your product group this year?

Customer: Well, we are supposed to achieve a 7 percent sales increase . . . but with the new competition we're facing from a much larger firm, any increase at all is going to be quite a challenge.

As soon as you hear information that may be useful, you will probably find yourself thinking, "How can my product or service help in this newly competitive environment? Do I need to ask more questions to try to find out how I might be able to help?"

Before you plunge into your solution, however, trust building requires demonstrating that you are listening to what the client has to say. If you can show your customers that you are really absorbing what they are saying, then you are showing them that they are really communicating with you. You are showing that you are customer focused.

You need to use body language to affirm that you are listening and absorbing what the client is saying. An occasional nod of the head, strong eye contact, alert head position, and erect posture tell the client you are absorbed in what she's saying. In person and especially on the phone, when the customer pauses, you may wish to say softly, "I see" or repeat a key phrase in a quiet voice. You don't want to stop the flow of conversation, but you want to let the customer know you are listening and to encourage her or him to continue.

Toward the end of the questioning process, start paraphrasing the prospect's concern(s). This has three benefits:

1. It demonstrates that you have been listening.
2. It gives the prospect a chance to confirm any concerns.
3. *It brings to the prospect's attention that there are problems, issues, and needs that must be resolved!*

This last point needs to be emphasized, because without needs, there is no point to your being there. *If the customer has no needs for you to fulfill, you are wasting your time!* In fact, in relatively rare cases you may decide that you can't really help the customer, in which case you should tell him or her and walk away from the sale. The occasional lost sale is not worth compromising your integrity. Actually, it will strengthen your integrity and character, and make you even more effective in helping the customers you can provide with good solutions. And if you are honest about the lack of fit between your company and the potential customer, that "lost" lead may refer someone else to you, if the occasion arises, simply because you were honest!

What Is the Prospect Willing to Do to Solve the Problem?

The prospect's needs or issues are now out in the open. By asking relevant, strategic questions, you have forced him to face these needs. There's no sense burying his head in the sand and pretending they don't exist! Now you need to encourage him to commit to a solution. Start by asking the customer what he thinks would solve his problem or satisfy his need.

By now you should have a clear picture of how your products or solutions may be able to help the customer, and you should be able to tailor your questions to hit on important points. Asking questions often overlaps with proposing solutions. In the Dialogue Box on page 105, the software consultant obviously knows that her product can increase efficiency and has tailored the question to hit that point—a point that is also the customer's primary concern.

Next, the salesperson must find out whether the prospect is serious about addressing his needs. More questions are needed. Is his problem large enough to invest in a solution? Will the return from his investment be worthwhile?

Congratulations. By asking questions, you have made the prospect admit his needs, face them, and commit to budgeting money to deal with them. Now, when you present your products or services, it won't be in a vacuum or in a "canned" presentation, but as a valuable solution.

When the Customer Talks, You're Selling

- When the customer talks, you are building rapport with the customer.
- When the customer talks, you are focusing on the customer.
- When the customer answers questions about his or her needs or desired solutions, you are moving toward a sale.

• • •

Listen, Then Affirm Concern

To build trust, show customers that you've been listening by using body language and repeating back what you think they're trying to communicate.

Salesperson: I hear you saying...

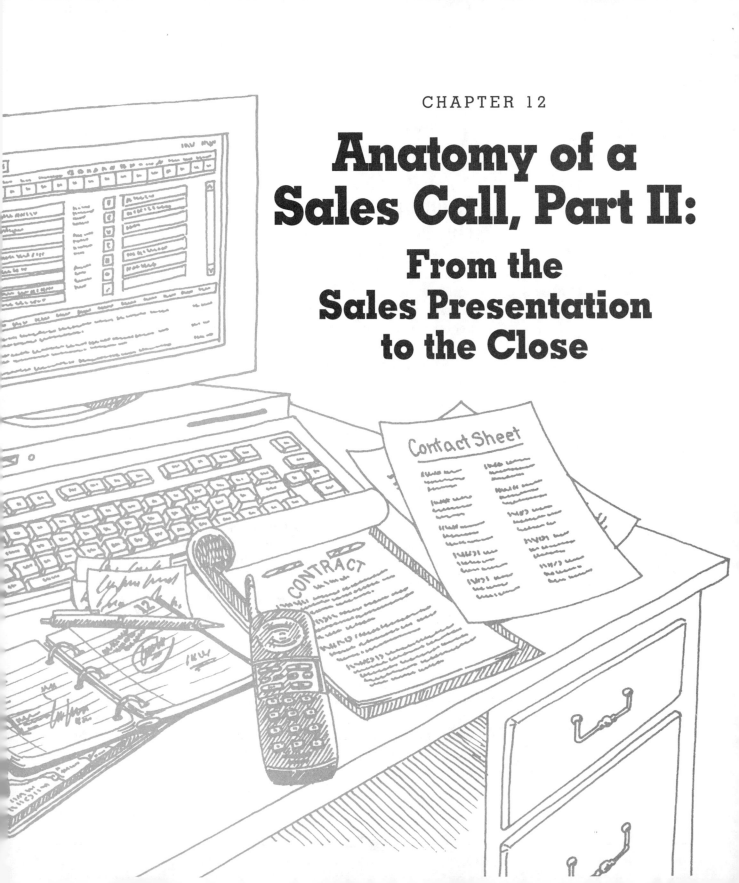

CHAPTER 12

Anatomy of a Sales Call, Part II:

From the Sales Presentation to the Close

Tailor Your Solution to Fit the Customer's Needs

As the sales rep, you add tremendous value by positioning your product to fit the customers' needs exactly. Let's say, for example, you are selling a machine that is strongly competitive in price, in performance, and in safety. Let's say, customer 1 is primarily interested in price. Fine. So for customer 1, you position your machine as being price-competitive. For customer 2, you position your machine first as being a strong performer. For customer 3, you position your machine first as being strong in safety. Of course, you need to be honest in this process. You don't want to say your machine is the lowest-priced alternative if it is not.

Once you and your client have agreed that there's a solution to be had for his problem, and that he has the money to invest in a solution, you need to show him how your product or service is the best solution for the money.

Tailoring a Solution to Fit the Client's Needs

Even very bright minds like to think in simple terms. Especially when we look at many similar or competing products or services, we like to be able to arrange them simply in our minds. Take cars, for example. People tend to associate one make of car with high performance, another make of car with luxury, another make of car with economy.

Similarly whatever product or service you are offering, your customers will tend to associate it with one particular benefit or feature. As a sales rep intimately familiar with the product, you probably don't see the product or service in such simple terms. But most customers buy lots of different products and services, and hence their minds tend to associate one major attribute with a particular product.

By taking the benefit or feature that matters most to the customer and focusing on that first, you are helping the customer sort out the confusing array of product or service alternatives from which they have to choose. Remember, the customer wants to buy. The customer wants to achieve a solution. By making it easier for the customer to see how your product or service can help achieve this solution, you—the salesperson—are helping the customer. (Appendix G contains a sample letter and questionnaire designed to help you structure an effective proposal.)

Presenting a Solution to the Client

Showing a customer why your company can provide the best solution for her problem often involves making a presentation. Here's where some of the sales tools from Chapter 1 will come in handy. Maybe you have a map that will help the customer visualize just what markets you cover—one of her key concerns. Or perhaps you have some testimonials from satisfied customers that will help build her confidence in your product or company. Maybe you have the results of a research study proving that the widget you manufacture is 20 percent stronger than everyone else's—and you know the prospect's main criterion for buying is the strength of the widget. Now is the time to walk the prospect through the sales tool kit, tailoring your presentation to her needs. She'll probably never read the information or understand it on her own, which is why you want to be the one to present the information to her!

If you've got some nifty sales tools, it can be awfully tempting to rely upon them to tell the story. Don't! You are the best person to tell the story and to tailor it to meet your client's needs. *Make sure you are not competing with your sales tools!* Don't pass out sales materials when you want people to focus on you. If you have a one-page complex diagram that you just have to show your customers, then pass it to the customers and let them focus on it. But if you really want them to focus on it, then don't talk while they are looking at it. Most of all, be cautious of handing your customers a big, glossy catalog with four-color pictures to look at while you want them to focus on what you have to say. Big, bright four-color pictures are interesting—and distracting—to flip through and look at even while someone is talking to you.

Using Sales Tools Effectively

One way to use sales tools effectively is to ask the prospect the very questions she's probably thinking, but not saying, aloud, while you are presenting them. "Why should this map interest you?" you can ask the client, while holding up the map in your tool kit. She doesn't know, so you tell her. "It should interest you because it shows that we really reach your target market." Get out a pen and write all over the map. Interact with the sales tools! Circle the spots the client is particularly interested in. Write down another fact that relates to the map and the client's needs but that isn't spelled out on the map.

If you feel compelled to include slides, videos, printed materials, or computer shows, don't let them overshadow you. Buyers can quickly lose patience with sales aids. They made an appointment

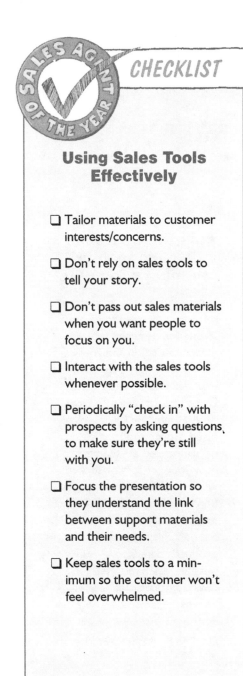

Using Sales Tools Effectively

❏ Tailor materials to customer interests/concerns.

❏ Don't rely on sales tools to tell your story.

❏ Don't pass out sales materials when you want people to focus on you.

❏ Interact with the sales tools whenever possible.

❏ Periodically "check in" with prospects by asking questions, to make sure they're still with you.

❏ Focus the presentation so they understand the link between support materials and their needs.

❏ Keep sales tools to a minimum so the customer won't feel overwhelmed.

Link the Customer's Needs to Your Product's Benefits

In presenting your products and services, you need to create a strong link between the customer's situation and your capabilities. Your job is to articulate that link, sharply and clearly. Don't just throw a lot of features at him. He'll just get confused. Concentrate on giving a highly focused presentation of how your product or service will definitively provide the solution he is looking for. Make sure he understands the link between his needs and your product's benefits. Wherever possible, ask him to tell you how a particular feature will help him. Remember, only the customer knows why your product is valuable to him!

with you, not with your sales aids. Their time is valuable, and they don't want to spend lots of time hearing about how great your product or service is. They want to know how it can help them address their individual needs.

Make sure in presenting solutions that you use a nice balance of the three primary tools: verbal, vocal, and body language. Use descriptive language and balance it with concrete examples of results. Go carefully and meticulously through how your product or feature clearly meets the primary concerns of the buyer, rather than quickly touching the surface of all your product's features. Involve your customers whenever possible. Check in with them by periodically asking questions to make sure they are with you every step of the way.

Asking for the Sale

Throughout the selling process you've explained to the buyer that you're not trying to get her to buy something she doesn't want, and you're not exaggerating or misrepresenting your goods or services. You've worked together with the customer on brainstorming a solution to her problem or need. Asking for the sale is the next logical step.

At this point in the sale, asking for the customer's business should really not be that difficult. All you have to do is tell the customer you'd like to move forward with the solutions you've just outlined and draw up a contract for sale.

If you have asked the proper questions and worked through the client's needs and solutions as I've just outlined, you and your customer should both be on the same wavelength. Ideally what should happen on at least some of your sales is that customers will signal to you that they are ready to buy. An example of a ready-to-buy signal is when the customer asks, "What's your availability for this?"

If you are telling the customer you'd like to move forward with the solutions you've just outlined and draw up a contract for sale, you might want to add, "Does that make sense to you at this point?" If the customer says yes, then you could say, "Let's take a look at the next steps" or "Let's outline the terms—your needs and our responsibilities."

"Never sign anything" is a standard piece of advice handed out to most people at some point in their life. No wonder closing can be so difficult. It brings up subconscious negative feelings. To avoid triggering these irrational, emotional, negative feelings, you need to be both straightforward and nonthreatening.

- *Avoid making a big deal out of the agreement process.* Avoid using words that may be scary to people, such as *legal, binding, final,* and *closing.*
- *Do use positive voice tone and body language.* Reaching agreement is an emotional time, so the feeling of trust is particularly important. You want to make sure customers know you are there to help them, and you are not going to disappear after the sale. Trust is largely generated by positive voice tone and body language.
- *Choose nonthreatening but straightforward words:*
  - "It sounds as though we have answered everything."
  - "Am I pretty much on target with this?"
  - "Should we move forward from here?"

Ask for the Sale

Give your client the opportunity to move forward down the road to success by telling her you'd like to move forward with the solutions you've just outlined and draw up the contract and related paperwork.

•••

Objections Are Buying Signs

If prospects don't raise objections, they're not really "buying" what you have to sell.

Once you have made the agreement statement or question, you want to get some kind of positive indication from the customer before you proceed. Don't go on if you just have silence.

You need something definite, such as "Yes, I'm with you," or at least a positive nod of the head. If you continue to move ahead without getting a positive signal, the customer may feel manipulated. Wait a few seconds. If you still don't get that signal, try to identify what is causing the hesitation.

If the customer appears in agreement, then outline the next steps. "So, we'll move ahead. The next step in this process is . . . " or "Let's each check our calendars and schedule the first planning meeting,

DIALOGUE BOX

Closing the Sale

Try transitioning to signing a contract with these statements:

"Let's take a look at the next steps."

"Shall we move ahead with this?"

"We seem to be in agreement that this solution would work for you. May we take the next step and draw up a contract?"

"Does it make sense to you at this point to draw up a contract?"

maybe in about two weeks." Lead them through how you will do business together. Don't appear overeager to get them to sign something—it's better to outline the next steps first. But do pull out the contract if the time has come for them to sign! By behaving matter-of-factly about the contract, you will soothe any fears the client may have about signing something.

By following this process, you and the customer should be at the same place when it comes to closing the sale. You should be thinking: "We're going ahead with this"—and the customer should, too.

Handling Objections

Prospects may raise objections during the fact-finding and brainstorming parts of the sale, or when you ask for the sale itself. Handling objections is one of the cornerstones of the selling process.

Objections are a natural outcome of brainstorming, and the only time you should be worried is when you *don't* get any objections from the prospect! Objections are buying signs. Instead of simply leaving, or asking you to leave, the prospective customer is presenting objections or reasons for not buying Objections show that the customer is considering using your product or service but isn't quite ready to go forward. Handling objections—answering the prospect's concerns—helps the buyer to feel that he has explored all possible issues and enables him to commit more fully to what you're selling. It also does another important thing: It rehearses him on how to handle objections he's likely to encounter when he presents your idea to the other bigwigs at his company or when the next salesperson comes into his office and asks, "Why would you do a stupid thing like buy from my competitor?"

Objections are temporary reasons for not buying, often because the prospective customer is either skeptical or unclear about your product or service. In many cases objections are simply the natural human tendency to avoid making a commitment. Remember, as children, most of us were taught "Never sign anything unless you're absolutely sure there are no hidden catches—and let the buyer beware!" As a result, even as adults, we all tend to hesitate to make the final commitment to buy a product or service even when we rationally believe we should. The objection by nature is something that can change, either with input from you or by your helping the prospective customer change his or her perspective about the objection.

For this reason, you should encourage the prospect to really consider her need and the possible solutions for that need. *You should encourage her to voice objections so you can deal with them.* An unanswered objection is a time bomb waiting to go off. The last thing you want to happen is to spend lots of time and energy working through a solution with the client and then have her go back to the office to "think about it," talk to a few people, and come up with some objection you haven't addressed. So when you do call back, she says, "Well, it sounded good at the time, but now that I've thought about it some more [or talked with the office manager, or a competing salesperson], I couldn't possibly do it because of [previously undiscussed objection]."

Some common objections include:

- "Your price is too high."
- "I want to think about it."
- "I have to ask my partner [brother, uncle, sister, dog]!"

By asking a lot of questions and really exploring a customer's needs, you've made it a lot easier to get past a buyer's objections. It's important to address the buyer's underlying concern, as opposed to replying to a knee-jerk response they are throwing out because they are uncomfortable buying for a reason they are not articulating. That's why learning to ask questions and to listen carefully to responses is so important. That's why confirming what you think the buyer is saying is so important.

The first key in managing objections is changing the way you hear them. Most buyers are conditioned to give out objections to salespeople when they aren't ready to buy. That's a buyer's right. However, too many salespeople take the objection at face value. Don't fall into that trap! Objections are very simply a *request* for something. Your real job is first and foremost to understand what the prospective customer needs from you. What, exactly, is he or

ATTITUDE ADJUSTMENT

Don't Be Afraid to Ask for the Sale

Many first-time sales people are afraid to ask for the sale. They hope that they won't ever have to bring it up, and that a contract will suddenly appear with the client's signature on the line. Alas, selling is not magic. You do need to ask for the sale.

And why not ask? There is nothing to be ashamed about here. You have just spent a good deal of your time assisting the customer in finding a solution for his or her problem. Your expertise and time are worth paying for.

Exercise:
Think of the times when you asked for something, and got what you asked for. Visualize the same success when asking for a sale. If you feel you are rarely able to ask for what you want, then begin practicing asking for what you want in your daily life. Start small if this idea is intimidating. For example, when your food arrives cold in a restaurant or the order is incorrect, send it back. Instead of putting any old piece of fruit in your shopping basket, take time to carefully pick out the *best* fruit. Graduate to asking a friend or family member to consider your needs.

Handle Objections, Rehearse the Client

When a prospect raises objections, be grateful! By raising objections, she is enabling you to coach her on how to deal with potential objections raised by other decisionmakers in the company or by salespeople who try to change her mind during the course of their sales call— when you're not around.

she requesting? This is a difficult mind shift; it means *listening* and *interpreting* rather than responding. This skill will take a little patience, a lot of self-awareness, and an increased ability to see beyond the words.

Discovering the Buyer's Real Message

The easiest way to identify the underlying request is to ask yourself what the prospective customer is requesting, what they really need to make this decision. For example, almost every sales rep at one time or another will hear that his or her "price is too high."

Taken at face value, the sales rep will usually respond by lowering the price. The customer got just what he or she wanted! Or did the customer? More likely, the customer is really saying, "I don't feel that what you are asking me to pay is what I perceive your product or service to be worth."

The real message is, The buyer is not convinced your product has any worth.

The "Price is Too High"

What the "price is too high" objection really means is that the customer is requesting a conversation about the *value* of your product or service and exactly how or why is it worth what you are asking the customer to pay. When you look at the objection as a request, there is plenty of opportunity to change the customer's perception.

The Objection-Handling Process

Once you have identified the "request," you are prepared to begin the objection-handling process. The premise of this process is that even during objections, selling is always collaborative. Selling through involvement will always serve you well, particularly in the area of objection handling. Remember, slow down and work the process; don't rush through to a quick close you're likely to lose.

1. *Listen.* Step one in objection handling is to listen. That might sound obvious, but now you know that what you are really listening for is the request. Take the time to hear the prospective customer out, even if you've heard that objection a thousand times before. Use positive body language to support the fact that you are listening rather than sending a message via body language that suggests you are preparing for a battle. Remember, this

Here are some of the most common objections we hear and their interpretation as a "request":

STATED OBJECTION	UNSTATED OBJECTION	THE REQUEST
Price too high	Cost vs. benefit	Value articulation
Need to think about it	Afraid to make a bad decision	Create comfort that this is the right decision
Get other quotes	Unsure you are meeting needs	Targeted solutions
All set with current supplier	Does not perceive you as better	Differentiation
Bad history	Bad experiences, sees you as them	Proof of improvements
Talk to my partner	Justifying a decision/unsure you are meeting needs Sometimes means you have not reached the decisionmaker	Risk reduction/articulate value Go back to square 1 and qualify your lead

Value What You Have to Offer

- My product or service is worth what I'm charging for it.

- I am convinced that they need my product.

- I am proposing a win-win situation.

- When the prospect puts money out into the universe, it comes back.

- You get what you pay for.

- There is enough money for us all.

- My proposal can help the prospect increase revenues.

- I am helping prospects sell their products.

- I am providing a valuable service for the client.

- I am offering the best solution at a fair and honest price.

- The prospect and I are a team and we need to share in the profits.

is a process, and together you and your prospective customer will be problem-solving the objection.

2. *Acknowledge/empathize.* Let them know that you heard the objection by acknowledging or empathizing. "So what I'm hearing is that you have some concerns with our price, is that correct?" or "I can understand that." Make sure that you don't jump on the band-wagon and confuse empathy with sympathy. Never make apologies or justify. At this point, keep it simple. If you tried to answer the objection at this point, the prospective customer wouldn't hear you; they are not ready to accept your ideas right now because they are still too attached to their objection.

3. *Ask questions.* The real power in handling objections is to uncover new information about the situation with good strategic questions. Those questions are very open-ended and investigative. Good starts include "Tell me about that" or "Could you elaborate on that for me?" Your goal here is to ask at least two probing questions to get the prospective customer talking. You are searching for a deeper understanding of the objection, involving the prospective customer in the process, and buying yourself some time to think.

4. *Summarize.* Once you've asked your investigative questions and the buyer has disclosed additional information, summarize it. Put it into precise format, especially if the customer has been talking at length. For example, "Let me just recap what I've heard. First, you're concerned with the pricing structure. Second, you have a limited budget for this project. And third, you need to make sure that this product is superior in quality because this is a high-profile project. Does that sound accurate?"

The prospective customer will either agree with you and be delighted that you actually listened, or will add additional facts to the list at this point. Once you have the client's agreement that you are on target with the concerns, he or she is ready to listen and you are prepared to talk!

5. *Answer the request.* Now that you have new information and you understand the request, you can effectively answer and handle the objection. Different objections call for different interventions or answers. In the example about price, a good start would be something like this: "You mentioned that this project is high-profile and that quality is essential. Let me share some additional information

with you that might answer both of those concerns at once . . . "
Now you can articulate value as it relates to your product or service
and the objectives. Here are a few guidelines on how to answer various objections:

> *They're skeptical.* Offer proof (testimonials, guarantees, case
> studies).
> *They misunderstood.* Offer information (in writing, descriptive, or
> third party).
> *There are real drawbacks.* Go to their original big-picture (mini-
> mize the drawbacks).
> *There are real problems.* Take action (describe what has or will
> change to eliminate it).

6. *Confirm agreement.* You are never done with an objection
until the prospective customer agrees that you're done. The only way
to make sure that the objection has been thoroughly answered is to
ask the prospect. This is a good time to be gentle and direct. Be
straightforward and ask the prospect, "Does that satisfy those concerns?" Then be quiet; let the prospect think it over and answer you.
If the answer is yes, congratulate yourself; you did a terrific job of
handling the objection with collaboration. If the answer is no or
"Yes, but I have some other concerns . . . " that's okay. Keep your
cool and go back to the beginning of the process and work the
model again.

It's also important to remind the customer that they do have a
problem to solve. Sometimes clients don't want to think about their
fears—and who does? The objections raised may also be the
prospect's way of denying the seriousness of their problem. For
example, using the "price" objection once again, everyone knows
"you get what you pay for." If the prospect does not believe her
problem is seriously impacting her business, she may not feel the
need to pay serious money to solve the problem. That's why it's
important when you hear an objection to return to re-examine the
prospect's need or issues and get her to acknowledge the severity of
the problem.

Don't give up; hang in there for the long run and you will close
many more sales. As you can see, this process is collaborative,

DIALOGUE BOX

Getting Past a Buyer's Objections

Here are some suggestions for getting past the buyer's hesitations.

- "You seem to be concerned
  about . . . "

- "I hear you saying that . . . "

- "Why is that important to you?"

- "What does that look like to
  you?"

- "How do you think [people at
  the client's company who will be
  affected by the decision to buy]
  will react to this?"

- "As I explained earlier, Mr.
  Decisionmaker, this meeting is
  all about coming up with a solution for your needs. Are you
  sure we've covered everything?
  Is there any need or problem
  that you have that you feel this
  solution won't effectively
  address?"

Overcoming Objections

Effectively overcoming objections is a four-step process:

❏ Show empathy, not sympathy.

❏ Probe to uncover additional information.

❏ Go back to big-picture objectives.

❏ Introduce new ideas and solutions.

• • •

The Objection-Handling Model

Here's the model:

❏ Listen

❏ Acknowledge/Empathize

❏ Ask questions

❏ Summarize

❏ Answer the request

❏ Confirm agreement

includes the prospective customer as part of the solution, and solves the objection thoroughly. It's the smart way to handle objections!

The same is true when the time comes to ask for the sale. By the time you are trying to finalize your agreement with the customer, you should have gotten the customer to the point where he wants to buy. If the customer is not at this point yet, you need to step back and figure out what is missing. Is he refusing to face his problem and the negative impact it's having on his business? Did you not show how the product's features will match the customer's needs? Did the customer raise a specific objection that you did not satisfactorily address? Is your timing off? Will you need to try to gain agreement during a subsequent sales visit?

Remember: You and the prospect are a team, working together to solve the prospect's problem with your solution. You should have the customer very close to agreement by showing how your products offer a solution and match the customer's need by overcoming any remaining objections. If you are not close to agreement, you need to step back.

Don't overlook a hesitation the customer has, either a hesitation that she verbally articulates or one that is expressed in body language. Identify any hesitation. Is there a particular objection that needs to be addressed? Is the customer still unclear how the product or service will really create a solution?

Filling out the Contract

If the customer decides to buy your product or service, you need to fill out the appropriate paperwork. Maybe it's a sales slip. Maybe it's a three-page contract with lots of tiny print on the back and triple carbons. Whatever it is, fill it out carefully and thoroughly and explain to the client what you're doing as you fill it out.

This may seem like a small point, but during my time as a sales manager I was handed numerous contracts that were poorly filled out or only partially filled out. By not taking the small amount of time necessary to fill out the contract correctly the first time, the salespeople caused problems down the

road. More than once they would have to call the customer back to fax them another contract with the information they *meant* to put down but didn't. Sometimes mere carelessness caused the problem, such as writing down the current year instead of a future date in the date line—a tiny detail, but it voided the whole contract! Sometimes a sales rep would list the final price, without listing discounts given for quantity or additional fees given for extra services—and the fact that the customer *did* receive the discount had to be explained all over again or the customer's complaint that he received "unexplained" charges on an invoice would have to be reviewed.

Remember to Breathe. Of course, everyone makes mistakes sometimes. Especially if you're nervous, you are likely to make an error. So, when it comes to filling out the contract, especially if you're not used to filling one out, take a deep breath and calm down. If you're worried that the customer will grow impatient while you're filling it out, follow the techniques outlined earlier.

By treating the contract in a matter-of-fact, casual, unhurried fashion, you are sending the message to the customer that the contract is nothing special, just a standard operating procedure. You are making the process of filling out the contract a non-threatening activity. By keeping the customer involved and explaining things as you go along, you are addressing the customer's possible fear that in filling out the contract you are "pulling the wool over her eyes" and trying to sneak through something he didn't agree to or bargain for.

Financial Commitment

You have almost finished closing the sale. You've settled on a price, gotten a verbal commitment, and drawn up the contract and presented it for signature. There's one important step that should not be forgotten—asking the customer to "put his money where his mouth is"!

Your company may have its own policy regarding payment schedules and credit. It goes without saying that it's best to be fully paid up-front. "Can you write a check now?" or "How would you like to pay for this—check or charge?" are the standard ways

Time Versus a Quick Buck

Lazy salespeople don't want to really sell the client. They just want a quick buck. They hear this objection and they cut their price to "get the sale over with." This attitude always backfires. First, because you haven't really sold the client based on the worth of your product, the client often doesn't come in when you do lower your price. Second, it backfires because you will have to sell more to make up for the price-cutting—and you will have to service what you do sell so you don't lose the clients you've sold. You won't be able to give the best service to these accounts, because you'll be too busy making up for lost revenue. And you'll resent having to provide service because you won't be getting paid a fair price to do so. You won't have any money left over to hire someone else to service the account. And you'll have a lot of account turnover—customers sold in this fashion—rather, who haven't been sold—have no real loyalty to you.

Heed the Buyer's Real Message

Only the buyer knows what she needs to hear in order for you to sell her. Objections are ways of telling the salesperson what needs aren't being met. The trouble is, objections don't always directly state what the customer's real issue is. The salesperson must listen carefully to the objection's subtext and probe carefully to hear the buyer's real message.

to handle this part of closing the deal. It's best to ask for the money in a matter-of-fact, almost casual way, as if you expect them to hand it right over—which you should, since you've spent so much time qualifying your customer as someone who is worthy to do business with!

If a customer has good credit, then your company may be willing to offer him or her a payment plan. Typical plans are half now, half when the deliverable is received, or a third up front, a third at delivery, and another third within thirty days of delivery. However, credit should only be offered the client when you are absolutely positive that the customer is credit worthy. If your company does not have a method for judging credit history, or if you are working on your own, then you can tell the customer that it is corporate policy to apply for credit with your company. To do so, they will need to fill out an application such as the credit accommodation form that is included in the forms appendix of this book. Once they have filled the form out, and given you permission to call the references listed on it, you can call the references yourself and get a sense of their credit rating.

Once you extend credit to a customer, the set dates for collecting the additional payments will serve to keep you in touch with the customer's needs, as well as get a sense of whether they are indeed credit worthy. If a customer pays one-third up front, for example, but balks at or widely misses your other payment deadlines, then that should be a warning for you to keep close tabs on them. It isn't worth your time and effort to sell something, maintain the sales relationship, and service an account that refuses to pay. Collections are difficult today, and can cost 30, 50, and up to 70 percent of the sales total. Frequently, companies can avoid collection altogether—for example, by closing one business and opening another under a different name. Don't fall into the trap of giving away stuff for free—get paid up-front or make sure a customer is credit worthy.

If you are operating a business on your own, it is worth calling your local law society or bar association and asking for an introductory meeting with a collections lawyer who can counsel you on collection issues.

Ending the Meeting by Planning for What Comes Next

Where do you go from here? At this point you and the client need to set an agenda for following up on the sales call. Maybe you didn't sell the client this time around, and you need to have a second meeting to present a formal proposal. Maybe you need to meet with other people at the clients' company. Maybe you need to meet with other people at your company to see what kind of offer you can make to the customer.

With the customer's input, make a "to do" list. Sometimes the customer will also have some things to do—to get you more information, or a spec sheet, or advertising materials. Whatever needs to be done, get agreement on it and write it down, so that you can do the necessary follow-up.

Next, it's time to conclude the meeting by assuring the client you'll follow through on their behalf, establishing a time frame for following through, and thanking them for their time: "It was great to go over things with you today. I'll get started on these items, and we'll probably talk again next week. Thanks once again for your time!"

Following Up

Not following up on a sales call is a primary reason for losing the sale and gaining dissatisfied clients. There are many reasons salespeople don't follow up on sales calls:

- They are disorganized, and either forget to follow up or lose sight of who they need to contact again.
- They're lazy, and they think it's the customer's job to follow up.
- They're overconfident, and they think they explained things so well during the meeting, they don't have to do any more work.
- They lack confidence, and are afraid the client will think they are being "pushy."
- Their enthusiasm slips after the sales call.

Sales Is a Process

Objections are just one step in the sales process. So when you hear one, you affirm to yourself: *This is a process, and together the prospect and I are brainstorming a solution to this problem. If I hang in here for the long run, I'll close many more sales.*

Keeping the Customer Involved

Verbally reviewing what you're doing as you write the contract keeps you on the same wavelength as the customer and confirms agreement. "Now, I just want to make sure I have the correct spelling of your name...the official name of your company...you did say you wanted package number two. Now that comes with, as I said, some extra items, so let me make sure I put that on the contract..."

- They are dishonest, and they say they'll do something when they won't.
- They get distracted, and by the time they remember they were supposed to follow up they think it's "too late," so they don't bother.
- It is too late.

Don't Deliberately Sabotage Yourself

Without exception, every sales presentation requires a follow-up. And you owe it to yourself to give the sale you've worked so hard at every chance of going through.

Proper follow-up can increase your sales 20 or 30 percent! Don't let your enthusiasm level slip after the sales visit. Follow-up calls take more energy than you might expect. Often the buyer, who probably sees salespeople constantly, may recollect your sales call more vaguely than you do. Don't be afraid to start selling all over again. Don't get frustrated! Don't give up! And keep on selling!

A prompt follow-up sends the message to the customer that he or she is important and not forgotten in all the activity. It says, "Thank you, I appreciate your business (or the opportunity for your business)."

Thank the Client

All the first follow-up contact after the meeting needs to do is to let the customer know that you plan on staying in touch. It's the first step in building a long-term relationship with the buyer, a relationship that perhaps may even lead to future referrals. Thank-yous are still something that everyone knows they should do, and that very few people actually do. Your objective, consistent with building your business, is to separate yourself from the crowd. A timely thank-you note or thoughtful telephone call still stands out as proper business etiquette after any important meeting. As I mentioned earlier, even keeping some postcards handy in your car to write a brief note on and post in the nearest drop box is a quick, painless, and very effective means of immediate follow-through. It's much better to get a handwritten note in a timely fashion than a typewritten letter months down the road, when the customer has forgotten all you've discussed!

Maintain Customer Contact

The sale does not end with the signing of the agreement. There always will be some concerns the customer has, even though he or she felt confident enough to commit to the product or service. These questions will likely be along the lines of:

- Whom do I contact if I have problems?
- Who will handle delivery and installation?
- Who will be my customer service contact?

These concerns should be reason enough to maintain supportive customer contact.

Keep the Client Informed

Whether it's a new trend in the industry, changing policies and staff at your company, or new services or products that your company is offering, you need to let your customer know about it. To build a long-term relationship with your customers, it is important to seize every opportunity to interact with them. In your ongoing business activities, try to seed reasons in your conversation for getting back in touch with each other sometime in the near future. These interim contacts are a good method to keep your relationship alive and to show your ability to follow through on what you say.

Develop an Active Follow-up System

Schedule customer follow-ups on a regular basis. This lets your clients know that you are part of their team and that you're committed to making their success your success. In addition, staying active with accounts keeps you in front of them. Your contact

CHECKLIST

Steps to Take to Follow Up after a Sales Call

- ❑ Thank the client after the meeting with a timely thank-you note or telephone call.
- ❑ Address customer concerns after the sale.
- ❑ Update the client with relevant news.
- ❑ Schedule customer follow-ups on a regular basis.
- ❑ Make sure your manner of follow-up—faxes, notes, and calls—reflects positively on you and reinforces your professionalism.

ATTITUDE ADJUSTMENT

Save Time— Do Things the Right Way

Sloppy paperwork will come back to haunt you—in the form of lost sales, wasted time re-hashing deals with the client, confusion in the accounting office, upset customers, and, last but not least, resentment on the part of your coworkers who have to handle your mess, resend invoices, or deal with bringing it to your attention—even if they don't share their (legitimate) resentment with you. Don't be arrogant! Filling out paperwork correctly will benefit you in the end and it takes very little effort to do it the right way.

doesn't always have to be in the form of addressing issues, as it can just as likely be signaling that you're there if they need you. Sending a copy of a trade article relevant to them or a thoughtful thank-you note may be just as meaningful; your actions can speak more than words. So, as important as it is to support the sales, use customer contact to distinguish you from your competitors, and demonstrate your commitment to and interest in being their provider of choice. Appendix G provides sample follow-up letters.)

Don't restrict your thank-yous to just after successful sales presentations. Follow-up actions should occur after every key meeting or event, including:

- Successful sales presentations and commitments
- Demonstrations
- Post-sale activities (for example, a notice of a change in intended shipping dates, or clarification of questions that come up regarding any of the miscellaneous details)
- Referrals
- Introduction of new products or service
- Account maintenance and relationship contacts

Remember: "Out of sight, out of mind." Keep in touch with your important customer base through periodic phone calls, newsletters, articles—anything available to let customers know that you are committed to a long-term partnership. If they continue to feel you are part of their team, at least in spirit, you'll reap the benefit of referrals that really makes this second effort pay off over the long run.

No matter what the method—telephone calls, letters, notes, e-mail, fax—execute it in a professional manner. Make the effort to purchase some quality business note cards and letterhead. When sending a fax, be sure to use a cover sheet and take the time to personalize your note. Whatever approach you choose, make sure it is a positive reflection on you and reinforces your professionalism. If in doubt about how best to keep in touch with customers, ask them how they would prefer future contact, and then make a note of it in your planner when entering the item.

CHAPTER 13

Understanding the Buyer's Personality

In the last few chapters, we walked step-by-step through a sales call, from getting an appointment to follow-up. In addition to basic information on sales etiquette (when to arrive, how to shake hands, etc.), there were some pointers on the psychological aspects of conducting a sale. We talked about why you should ask questions—how focusing on the customer's information, not your own, engages the customer more fully in the sale—and the benefits of conducting a sales call as a problem-solving "brainstorming" session answering a customer's needs.

In this chapter, we'll look at the psychological aspects of selling in more detail. No one sells in a vacuum. Remember, "A buyer doesn't buy from a company, but a person." The converse is true as well: "A seller doesn't sell to a company; a seller sells to an individual, or group of individuals." Each interaction in the selling process takes place between two different people or groups of people. Even in very large corporations, where strict guidelines are written and enforced to control the buying and selling process, the human dimension can't be overlooked.

So, although brainstorming a solution for the customer provides you with a very sound foundation for sales, it isn't always enough. Often the success of a sale hinges on nuances of personality and personal style that exist outside the usual business parameters. As a salesperson, you need to go beyond the obvious—understanding the sale in terms of what it does for the customer—to understanding the buyer's personality style, and then take this into account as you work with the customer. You'll be even more successful in your sales presentations when you work at two levels—addressing both the buyer's *business* and *personal* priorities.

Understanding the buyer's personality helps you figure out:

- How to approach a particular buyer
- What the buyer's reactions to your product or service will be
- What the buyer is really looking for—including any "hidden agendas"
- What objections the potential buyer is predisposed to raise to your presentation
- What sort of things will make the buyer comfortable with proceeding

- The best approach to use when trying to get a buyer to commit

Six Basic Prospect Types

People are very complex, and one thing you'll discover in selling is that they will continually surprise you. Having said that, most buyers are likely to fall into one of six categories. If you can identify the category, then you can figure out how to best handle the prospect:

1. The Fact-Checker

This skeptical individual prides himself or herself on making sound business decisions based on fact. In many ways, this is one of the easiest types of customers to sell to, because they tend to be very rational. If you can supply them with facts and figures then you are on your way to a sale. Some ideas include:

- An independent study showing your product or service performs better than the rest
- Proof you reach a larger market than others
- Testimonials verifying customer satisfaction
- A positive mention or review in a newspaper article, magazine, or trade association newsletter

2. The Cold Fish

This category consists of indifferent individuals who appear completely detached from the outcome of the buying process, and from the process itself. The cold fish is one of the toughest types to do business with. Often, they don't have pressing needs—at least, none that they're willing to admit—and they act as if they could care less about your product or offer. The information-gathering approach discussed so far offers you something of a chance of success with this type, because cold fish are only likely to buy from someone with whom they feel they have a relationship. Relationship building and finding common ground is all important with this type

of client! Ask yourself, how can you create a relationship? Do you or can you belong to the same clubs, support the same charities, or share a common interest in collecting Art Deco furniture?

3. The Dazed and Confused Type

This customer, as the rubric implies, hasn't "got a clue." They know very little about their business or industry, and they certainly don't know how to make a decision that will benefit their company! It's up to you to gently point out the questions they should be asking and to supply them with the answers—answers that also explain why your product or service is best. Make the best choices for these clients in the context of a warm, nurturing educational presentation, and they will be very grateful for your help!

4. The Servicee

This type of buyer understands their business, and may even know how to make the right choice—whatever you're selling. But before they buy, they want to make sure you're going to fulfill their biggest need both before and after the sale—maid service. They need lots of attention, often for nitpicky things. They may change their mind frequently, asking you to redo their order over and over again, call you repeatedly with the same questions, or ask for your input on things that don't relate directly to the sale. Sometimes, they just want to talk, exhibiting an extreme need for attention. They want you to make them feel important—as important as any international VIP, even if their order is the smallest one on your list. Ask yourself, how can you service this person without going bankrupt on time and energy? How can you set appropriate boundaries, without making them feel slighted?

5. The Battering Ram

In this category we find those customers who are crude, rude, demanding, critical, and, unfortunately, sometimes nasty. In their culture, they are admired for their open "I say what I mean, I tell it like it is" personality and because they'll "never let someone pull the wool over my eyes." Sometimes, however, they are bullies masquerading as grownups whose agenda is to batter salespeople into giving them what they want at any cost—or because it makes

1. *Driver.* From a sales perspective, driver personalities tend to be the most challenging because they are difficult to build rapport with. All business people who exhibit the driver social style are generally very controlling in their approach to others. They are bottom-line oriented and want to talk about results. You'll recognize drivers because they speak in bullets and tend to be forceful and extremely direct. Their body language is characterized by a forward lean. On the plus side, their directness makes it easier to have your proposal judged on its merits, with little distraction caused by irrelevant relationship or political factors. To handle the driver, clearly define your purchase justification. Use facts and figures to document your case. Move briskly through your sales presentation. Let them be the boss.

2. *Analytical.* The analytical personality typically comes across as a "thinker." The thinker is very process oriented and tends to like facts and figures. They are systematic and thorough in their decision making. Usually they are quite reserved and not too outgoing. During your sales presentation they tend to avoid eye contact. The traditional approach of looking the customer in the eye will backfire. This direct approach will make them look away and withdraw their attention. Understand it isn't you, it's a style difference. Thinkers are less talkative and much more thoughtful than other personality types. They're going to try to analyze everything you tell them. To communicate with this personality, be accurate and precise in your supporting documentation. Back up your case with facts. Move slowly through your presentation, and don't be aggressive.

3. *Amiable.* "Relationship" is the key word for people with an amiable social style. They're cooperative, friendly, easygoing people. They don't like conflict and don't respond well to pressure. Getting this buyer's attention is often easy, but getting them to make a decision is difficult. They are susceptible to "buyer's remorse," wherein their unease with making a decision will cause them to change their mind shortly after you've left the office. Be cautious selling to this style of individual. Work carefully through your sales presentation. Take a few minutes and chat first, making them feel important, before moving on. Give them plenty of attention. Proceed slowly and let them talk. Take time to build a relationship with them so they feel they can trust you. Once you have their trust, providing them with guarantees (as long as you can follow through on them!) will help sway the sale in your favor.

4. *Expressive.* Expressive people tend to be extremely outgoing. They are big-picture operators with lots of body language and facial expressions. They like to tell stories and be onstage. When presenting to them, sit back and become a very good listener. Let them pontificate about everything that's important to them. Be careful not to go into too much detail; they are easily bored. Rather, appeal to them in terms of how you are addressing their concerns about the big picture, and how your product or service will have a tremendous impact on their business. React positively to their ideas—be an interested audience, then give them a fast-paced presentation supported with testimonials.

them feel powerful! Just holding a conversation with this type of prospect can make you feel as though you're engaging in war.

Your first response should be to disassociate the person's behavior from you. Cultivate detachment. It may be that this individual is just used to communicating in a more brusque style than what you're used to dealing with. *Don't get offended.* Instead, listen to what he or she is saying, all the while reminding yourself that the way it's being said has *nothing* to do with you.

On the positive side, these individuals are blunt about what they want and what it will take to make a deal. If you can give them exactly what they want at exactly the time they need it, you're in luck. If not, then the challenge is getting them to change their mind about what "deal" they want. Asking them questions can help them understand why your service or product offers them the best deal.

If the individual is arrogant and hostile, it is still important to listen. Listening and repeating back to the prospect what he or she says to you can help diffuse the hostility. Does this person have a just gripe? Perhaps they had a bad experience with someone from your industry before or a previous salesperson from your company. Can you provide a new solution? Can you ask him or her to clean the slate and "start over" again with you? If the answers to these questions is yes, then move forward.

True bullies are a bit more difficult to handle. These people are often two-year-olds masquerading in adult bodies, testing you until you lose patience. Some bullies will only respect you if you show them you won't be intimidated by them: you'll need to be very blunt about what you can and cannot do and what you will and will not put up with. In some cases, they become lambs when you "bully" them back! If you do not want to meet them on their own turf, as it were, then perhaps your time is better spent cultivating other clients. In a worst-case scenario, Battering Rams can never be satisfied and dealing with them will drain you of energy better spent elsewhere.

6. The Insider

In many ways the ideal client, the insider is interested in what you have to offer. He or she totally buys what you have to say about the sale being a win-win situation and the two of you working together to brainstorm a solution. This person wants to feel part of your organization! Insiders want to be a part of your big picture. So build them into the big picture and help them see themselves as part of your company's group of smart, successful people "in the know." Ask them to contribute a tidbit to your newsletter. Write them up in the "people in the news" section. Let them know about promotional events you're putting on; ask them to help. Insiders are the most likely candidates for giving you a referral. Ideally, you want to convert every client to Insider status!

Of course, people are rarely true to only one type. Most people are hybrid personalities—a little bit of this, and a little bit of that. Still, by being aware of which type they're coming from, you can make your response to their questions and concerns much more effective.

KEY IDEAS

Resist to Persist

Often clients do not want to acknowledge their needs. Why? It gives you, the salesperson, power over them. And they don't want to be in the power of the salesperson! That's why they may resist answering questions, too. In asking questions, you need to be as nonthreatening as possible and explain that you are just trying to understand their situation better to see if there's any way you can help them—or not. Once you know that they have a problem, and that it's one you can help solve, there is no benefit to downplaying the need. Rather, you need to encourage prospects that, while they do indeed have a serious issue to resolve, you're sure you are the one who can help them solve it.

CHAPTER 14

Twelve Top Sales Approaches

Don't Bash the Competition

Do seek information about what your competition is doing. But don't bash them! No one enjoys hearing negative comments about other business-people, and bashing your competition destroys trust.

This chapter presents the basic sales approaches that professionals find most helpful. If you've had little experience selling, you should start by memorizing these approaches and experimenting with them on individual sales calls. For example, choose the one approach that is most likely to apply to the customer with whom you're working and stick to it throughout the call. As you gain more experience, you may mix and match these techniques throughout the course of a sales call, coming up with a hybrid selling approach that is custom-tailored to the client at hand and suits your unique personality as well.

Remember, no matter what technique you choose, use it within the context of information gathering for solutions and brainstorming outlined in previous chapters. Otherwise, the selling process is likely to degrade into the equivalent of an exchange of gunfire between two battleships: you firing a volley of reasons to buy, such as a great product or service features or today's special offer, and the customer firing back a volley of objections and reasons not to buy. That's what happens when the two of you haven't explored what information is really meaningful to the client. The selling approaches listed here are useful tools, but they won't replace a larger, in-depth search for the customer's true needs and the value your product or service provides in fulfilling them.

1. Focusing on Product Features and Benefits

Perhaps the most common sales approach, product-focused selling highlights product or service features. Each product has its selling points. Even sales reps selling inferior products or services can always find some positive selling points. If you have explored the customer's concerns, and determined that he or she is most interested in product features, as opposed to service, reliability, or some other concern, then this is the approach to try. However, there is a right way and a wrong way to go about presenting product features.

The Wrong Way.

"Our new industrial engine has 270 horsepower, 12 cylinders, 18 valves, and a 24-month guarantee." A basic problem with this approach is that the buyer may not care! Which feature is the customer really interested in? Just because the last customer cared about horsepower doesn't mean this customer will. An even more serious problem is the buyer may not even be listening! People who make buying decisions often hear one sales rep after the next roll off product features and attributes. Maybe an hour before, another sales rep began her presentation with "Our new industrial engine has 275 horsepower, 14 cylinders, 16 valves, and a 30-month guarantee."

The Right Way.

Link benefits to product or service attributes the customer cares about. Ask the customer, "If you had a product that had this [feature, e.g., eighteen valves], would it be helpful to you?" then try to discuss why or why not. This way talk about product features develops naturally from interacting *with* the client instead of being arbitrarily forced *on* the client.

2. Selling Against Your Competition

Everyone has competition, and at some point, you'll have to deal with yours. One way to deal with competition is to not focus on it. For example, you could say: "Company X is a good company, but we offer something quite different." This encourages the buyer to hear about your product while sidestepping a head-to-head comparison of your product with Company X's version. Of course, it only works if what you have to sell, while covering the same bases as what Company X has to sell, does indeed have many more different features or services, offers a larger market, or in some other way stands out from the competition.

One of the fastest ways to alienate your prospective customer is to start bashing your competitors or their products. Even if you are completely right, customers don't enjoy hearing negative things about other firms. Saying negative things can ruin any ability to build trust. Are you going to trust someone who has lots of negative things to say about

An Unprofitable Business Can't Help Anyone

Keep in mind that trades, discounts, and free trials are ways to *begin* working with a client, but they will not pull in the income necessary to run a profitable business. Your goal should always be to get the full price. Even while you're arranging for a "deal" or price cut, you should be selling the client on an all-cash sale the next time around.

Save Time—Organize Accounts by Industry

To make the most of your selling time, you can organize your sales campaign by concentrating on just one industry. The benefit of doing this is that you'll be able to concentrate your resources on making contacts, networking, and learning about one industry at a time.

their competitors? Probably not. It is far better to allow the prospect to do his own thinking on the subject. Chances are that the customer knows the negatives about your competitor's product, service, or business better than you do. If you ask him whether a particular service or need is important to him, and he knows he's not getting it, and you can show him that you offer it, he will do his own internal comparison. Making any negative reference about any product or service the customer has previously bought is indirectly criticizing his or her judgment.

You can, however *seek information* by asking, "What are they doing for you? Did it work? What can I do for you?" One way to build trust *and* sell against your competition is to say positive things about your competitors. "Yes, Company X does a good job of [service feature]. Let me tell you what we do in that area."

Today, as a matter of policy, many astute salespeople and businesses even go so far as to refer some business to their competition when they think it might be in their customer's best interests. For example, suppose you know you can't meet a customer's scheduling requirement. A printer I once used could not meet a scheduling requirement that I had for my magazine, and my sales rep went out of the way to find a printer who had an opening in his schedule that did meet my need. I took the opening, but went back to my old printer for the next issue. Why? The new printer treated me like a one-time customer, and didn't attempt to convert me to a permanent customer. The old printer cared more about my needs. Rather than forcing me into a situation that wouldn't work for me, my rep found another solution. Afterward, they were eager to get me back and to work hard to prevent the scheduling fiasco from happening a second time.

3. Selling by Addressing the Prospect's Competition

The prospect also has competition, and for every thought you have about dealing with your competition the prospect has a thought about her own. What are they doing? Are they offering something better than I am? Are they doing something that I'm not doing that works? What are they saying about me? Are they more successful

than I am? What are they doing that I should be doing? What can I do to match or better their numbers?

If you are working within a particular industry, chances are you will be trying to sell both to the prospect and to her competition. Don't give into the prospect's asking for proprietary information about her competition. Maintain your integrity by offering general information about the industry at large. If you are willing to tell her about her competition's secrets, what's stopping you from sharing the prospect's secrets with the competition? Stay out of trouble, and don't do it. Focus instead on the prospect's issues and concern and what you can do to help her without playing favorites.

Many customers want to be seen where their competition is, yet others want some kind of exclusivity from their vendors. You may be in the position to provide exclusivity—or you may not be. Chances are if you aren't, your competitor won't be in the position to, either. Assure the prospect who asks for exclusivity that every client of yours gets the "gold" treatment and that you'll do everything you can to service their needs and proceed to find out what they are so you can do just that.

4. Selling on Price

Selling isn't always easy. And there's nothing wrong with telling a prospective customer about any legitimate sales incentive that will help make the product or service more attractive—including price. It's usually very easy and quick to explain to the customer the value of a sales incentive like a one-thousand-dollar factory-rebate check. The problem is, no matter what the customer says about wanting a better price, giving him one doesn't always result in a sale, or in a positive customer relationship.

Chapter 13 already presented some of the problems with selling based on price. No matter how generous the "extra" sales incentive is, keep your primary focus on how the product or service is going to deliver a solution for the customer. Even if you are offering a 50-percent-off sale, a "buy one, get one free" offer, or a thousand-dollar factory-rebate check, you first should show the customer how you are going to deliver a solution. Then at

Focus on What You Can Do, Not on What the Competition Is Doing

Dwelling on your competition also conveys the impression that you are threatened by them. It tells the prospect that she may have a good reason to consider going with the competition.

Avoiding the Pitfalls of a Price War

❏ Always sell your product first.

❏ Use price reductions as "bonus" benefits—not as the primary benefit, which should be to address the customer's needs.

❏ Offer the price rebate for a limited time only, and stick to the deadline; it lets customers know you mean business and may make them more eager to act the next time you offer "a deal."

❏ Get something from the client in exchange for a price reduction, because this teaches the customer the ultimate value of your product. For example, you can discount the value of your product in exchange for a trade of goods or services equal to the discount. Perhaps the client has something you can use and will supply you that item in exchange for deducting its cost from the cost of the item you're selling.

the appropriate time you can use the incentive to help move the sales process to the agreement stage. Few people buy things just because they are on sale. Most of us have at least some interest in what the product or service can do for us.

Selling on price can backfire in other ways. If you are able to set your own rates and if you cut your rate so low that you can't afford to service clients well, you are heading for disaster. You won't be able to follow through on your promise, and you'll destroy your customer relationship. If you cut your rate without convincing the customer that she's getting a great deal, she won't value what you're selling her, and will find it surprisingly easy to pay somebody else more because she perceives the value of the competitor's item to be greater than yours. After all, you came down so quickly in price, you obviously know your product isn't worth much, right? Last, but not least, if you cut your rate, you may very well find that the client will refuse to pay a higher price at a later date.

A lot of salespeople think that discounting speeds a sale along. With rare exception, nothing could be further from the truth. All true "sales" go through the same process. No matter what features, benefits, or price you offer, you will have to go through that process if you want to establish a strong, long-term relationship with that customer. And that takes time. So you need to give the overwhelming emphasis to solving the customer's needs, even when you also have a juicy sales incentive to offer.

5. Selling by Categories

Selling by categories is an approach to consider when you have an item or service that can be sold to different industries. For example, perhaps you represent office equipment. As a salesperson, you could theoretically approach banks, garden centers, and retail stores with your products. Even though these

three businesses are very different, each one would have a reason to buy office equipment.

Selling a single category can benefit you in other ways. Suppose you have a product that is a marginal need for a particular industry. If you can offer that industry something special, you may provide a bonus source of revenue for yourself. Magazines and newspapers do this all the time with special sections called "advertorials." They'll identify one group of products, for example, the real-estate industry, and market a "special section" in the publication in which they group all real-estate ads and run special copy that talks about why and how to invest in real estate from the advertisers' point of view. Advertisers grumble about being placed next to their competitors, but often they'll scramble to be in the section for the same reason—they want to appear where their peers are.

You can take this same concept and use it creatively to promote very different products. Let's say you sell a makeup line primarily to women through at-home parties. There is nothing to stop you from typing up a one-page "newsletter" about the importance of looking professional at work and tailoring the presentation to female office managers, then having an event "Professional Makeovers for the Female Office Manager" in a local room at your library and inviting this special group of individuals to attend. In this way, you start to grow your business through a special sales category.

Although concentrating on a single industry has merit, two things may happen if you put all of your eggs in one basket. First, you might exhaust possible prospects in your particular areas; and second, if the economy hits that particular industry hard, you'll be hard-hit, too.

6. The Soft Sell

The classic soft sell is just leaving the customer with some information and letting them get back to you if they are interested. It is rarely effective for either you or the customer, because you haven't bothered to find out what her needs are and worked through them to find a solution. You aren't really doing your job! Usually your customers are not going to seriously consider buying your solution unless you help show them how it might be able to help them.

KEY IDEAS

Save Time—Organize by Category

Preparing an overview of categories to approach and then going after them in an organized fashion can give your sales effort a breadth and diversity that may provide a more stable customer base in the long run, depending on your industry. For example, if you sell a particular computer program, you can concentrate on selling it to banks first, hospitals next, and schools later on. This will keep you more efficient because, instead of learning about several different industries at once and networking three different groups of people at the same time, you can concentrate on one.

Fear of Selling

Few people like a pushy sales-person. There is nothing wrong with a "soft" approach, one that is based on information gathering and mutual solution finding. But there is something wrong with the sales-person who feels compelled to sidestep the selling process alto-gether!

Remind yourself that you are here to help the customer. Your client deserves help, and you deserve to be paid for your ser-vices. It's your job to move through the entire selling process, including discussing a budget and asking for the sale. Anything less is not doing your job, which is to serve the client's best interests!

Affirmations:
❏ *I am selling a service that meets needs.*
❏ *I am providing a valuable profes-sional service.*
❏ *Just as a doctor fixes a broken leg, I am fixing my client's [faulty marketing scheme, broken parts, etc.].*
❏ *My professional services are sup-plied for a fair and honest fee.*

Related to the classic soft sell are those approaches in which salespeople position themselves as something other than salespeople. They confuse the prospect by discussing promotions or "freebies," as in the case of an advertising salesperson for a magazine pre-tending to be an editor. This approach has little value. Besides, con-fusing the customer, you may create an unhappy client when the prospect discovers he has to pay for something and then feels misled and cheated. Also, you can spend a lot of time with the client—in effect, waste a lot of time—and lose the possibility of making future sales to this client in the process.

7. Selling with Fear

This sounds like a negative way to sell. You, like most people, prob-ably don't like to think about negative things, and may even want to skip this section. Don't!

It's true that if your sales pitch is based on fear, you may find it difficult to get prospective customers to listen. Telling the prospect that buying your product is the only way to beat her competition may scare her but it won't make her trust you.

On the other hand, if there's a real threat to her business that she is refusing to address because of her own fears, your job is to empower her to come up with good solutions to the problem. By drawing out her fears, you can address them with a solution that will provide relief. No one likes to get sick, but everyone should be grateful to the physician who diagnoses an illness correctly and then figures out a "cure"! You, too, are a doctor, diagnosing ills and pro-viding cures. Paint the picture of the strong feeling of confidence the prospect will have knowing that she made the right decision to address her need or problem with a solution she knows will work! To really succeed in selling, you want to provide your customers with a positive service, not just by selling them a good product or service that really meets their needs, but also by making the sales process as honest, open, and positive an experience as it can pos-sibly be. The customer will feel better. You'll feel better about your-self. And in the end, you'll make more sales.

8. The "We're Good Friends" Sell

One of the biggest myths in sales is that the customer is your friend. The customer is not your friend. The customer, for all of the reasons already outlined, is interested in having his needs met; and when it comes to his needs or yours, he will choose his needs. I hope that is not your definition of friendship!

Throughout the selling process, you need to keep in mind that you are in a professional relationship with the buyer. Protect yourself and your company by making sure all paperwork is filled out and all criteria are met along the way—no exceptions! I once had a client who was so friendly, she invited me to her house for dinner more than once. I even attended a Christmas party at her parents' house. Soon after, she called me to say she was going out of business, but would pay me what she owed in a few months. Needless to say, she never did—and never responded to numerous messages left on her answering machine. Some friend! I never heard from her again.

If I had been more experienced in sales, I would have insisted she send me a personal note guaranteeing that she would pay me within ten days, or that, regretfully, company policy would force me to file in court. I didn't do that, and lost a lot of money—and a friendship as well!

Having said all this, people do like to buy from other people they feel they have something in common with. That's one of the reasons as a salesperson you should dress in tune with the people you're calling on, join the clubs they join, and socialize where they tend to socialize. Networking is one means of cultivating friendly relationships with potential customers. Keep in mind that you should nurture a friendly relationship with potential and current customers, slowly. Buyers are defensive and quickly shrug off a salesperson who is overly friendly, especially at the early stages of building a business relationship. Keep the small talk short, and be sure that you quickly progress to a business discussion focused on helping your customers build their business. Show customers that you care by servicing their needs and sending them an occasional thoughtful note, or presenting them with a customer appreciation plaque, rather than buying elaborate presents. (Customers don't like to feel as if they are being "bribed.") Practice common sense in your business "friend-

CHECKLIST

Ways to Maintain Your Integrity

- ❏ Don't reveal proprietary information.
- ❏ Don't play favorites.
- ❏ Don't promise what you can't deliver.
- ❏ Don't cave in to unreasonable demands.
- ❏ Focus on delivering solutions to customer problems.
- ❏ Don't expect quick, easy results.
- ❏ Assure prospects that every client of yours gets the "gold" treatment.
- ❏ When you can, put your "promises" and "expectations" down on paper, so there's no misunderstanding.
- ❏ Have a superior review written promises before you agree to deliver them; if that's impossible, wait a day and review them when your head is "clear."
- ❏ Articulate company policy—and stick to it.
- ❏ Prepare a company policy sheet on commonly asked questions or demands to support your discussions.
- ❏ Don't take sides; engage choices and review priorities when there are conflicting points of view in a discussion, so the needs of all sides are heard.

Play Up Your Company's Reputation

You also can use your company's reputation to help you sell by directly referencing it when you can tie it to the customer's needs. You can refer to it indirectly though sales materials (a "company backgrounder" or a newspaper article referencing your company as a leader or expert in its field). You can refer to it directly by speaking firsthand about what you admire about your firm, boss, or job—businesspeople work hard to keep their own employees satisfied, so they are often favorably impressed when they meet an employee of another company who likes his or her job. Your job satisfaction sends a message that the company operation is sound and you are likely to be servicing their account for some time to come.

ships" by maintaining a positive attitude and refusing to say negative or disparaging things about other people. People feel empowered when they are with people who appear to have their act together, so avoid discussing personal or business problems with clients.

9. Selling on Reputation

Your reputation is one of the most powerful sales tools you have, so guard it well. Maintain your personal integrity by doing what you say you will do and not promising to deliver what you can't. In other words, "walk your talk." Playing fair with everybody, rather than playing favorites, will benefit your reputation in the long run.

The key to making a reference to reputation useful is to always put it in the context of the customer's issues. If the customer is looking for one-on-one service, then assuring the customer that your company is one of the world's megacorporations is probably not going to help you make the sale. The customer may think, "They're too large to pay attention to little old me." Or the client may assume that you're more focused on continuing to build your company and your own accomplishments than on helping your potential customers build their company. Let's say you are a management consultant trying to sell your services to a small business. If you go out of your way to mention that you have an M.B.A. from Harvard and worked on Fortune 500 accounts at a major accounting firm, you just don't know if you're going to be impressing your prospects or alienating them. Do they respect people with a master's degree? Do they want someone with a lot of big-company experience?

Having said that, it has been my experience that most people out there want to "go with the flow." We are a nation of copycats, not individuals. People will often come right out and say that they want to be with the "big company," whether or not that company serves them best. They want to "be where everyone else is." If you are a small company, this can be difficult to combat. However, it's not impossible. Through your in-depth questioning, the customer may discover that he or she is not being served the best way possible, and that your smaller company offers more. You can use referrals and testimonials at appropriate times to build the prospect's sense of a community of people who have not only bought your product, but have found that working with you is a sound business decision.

Whatever your situation, relying just on reputation to sell puts you at the risk of being seen as someone who really doesn't care about the prospective customer, but only wants to make the sale. To make this approach work for you, wait for signals from prospects that they are interested in hearing about your firm, and keep the focus on the customer, not on you or your company.

10. The Problem-Solution Sell

The problem-solution sell goes like this: The customer raises a problem, and you provide a solution. Many times, this sell depends on being able to overcome the prospect's objections.

When you're first starting out, there is nothing wrong with having a list of possible responses to objections or problems that need to be solved. Knowing what to say will make you feel more confident; and if the responses are appropriate, they can even help you sell. However, all too often a salesperson responds to objections or problems with a rote answer that sets up a dialogue of opposites with the buyer. The danger is that the problem-solution or objection-response dialogue can devolve into an argument between buyer and seller. You are unlikely to convince the prospect to buy from you, even if all of your responses to his or her problems are perfectly rational.

Salespeople fall into this trap when they try to close the sale before the customer has really decided to buy the product or service. Customers will find one objection after the next—or one problem after another—if they are not completely comfortable with making the purchase.

11. The Consultive Sell

The consultive sell is the problem-solution sell in a much more palatable guise. In this approach to selling, the salesperson questions buyers thoroughly to find out what their real needs are, and then gets the buyers to describe their ideal solutions. The salesperson

Prepare for Objections

Many new salespeople are stymied the first time they hear an objection or a problem. They haven't heard it before, and they don't know how to answer. This is a scary experience. You certainly don't want the client to think you're an idiot.

For this reason, many sales managers provide beginning salespeople with a list of suggested responses to commonly made objections. For example:

Customer: I can't afford it.
Salesperson: You can pay in twelve installments.

Exercise: Make a list of possible objections and your response to them.

---

acts as a facilitator to the process, and offers expertise when the buyer signals he or she is ready for a solution. The consultive sell is the method that's been discussed throughout this book, and it is the method preferred by most sales "consultants" today.

In the consultive sell, no immediate "solution" is offered by the salesperson in response to the "problem" described by the client. The point of the consultive sell is to assist the prospect in creating his or her own solutions and providing solutions that work when the prospect is ready for them.

12. The Added-Value Sell

Many clients today expect a lot from their providers—more than the actual product or service. Even if clients don't expect anything "extra," providing them with "added value"—worthwhile services above and beyond the actual item being sold—will distinguish you from the crowd.

For example, let's say you see a car at Showroom A and a car at Showroom B that you like equally as well. Why would you choose one car over the other? Well, perhaps Showroom A has a better service department. They'll pick up your car and drop it back at your house, free of charge, anytime you need to get it inspected or repaired. With Showroom B, you have to ask somebody for a ride to and from the car dealer. The added value that Showroom A offers is likely to sway your decision to purchase the car from them.

More complex products and services naturally lend themselves more easily to the opportunity to provide extra value, as do large corporations with extensive support staff. But smaller companies and individual salespeople can do a lot, too. Sending out a newsletter outlining industry trends, giving out promotional materials the client can provide to customers to stimulate business, providing leads through mail-in cards, or offering to do in-house demos as your customer's place of business are all ways you can build "added value" into your sale.

CHAPTER 15

Selling to Multiple Buyers

Now you know a lot about individual customers, but what happens when you have to sell to more than one person at a time?

Step 1: Meet the Individuals

All groups are made up of individuals. The first thing you need to do is to meet those individuals. After you are introduced, ask if you may go around the room and find out who each person is and what they do. You'll use all of the information you have so far to quickly discover what personality types you're dealing with and what each person's role is in the decision-making process.

Step 2: Determine Who the Group Leader Is

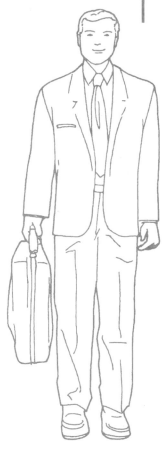

There may appear to be someone who is the leader. This person is managing the meeting, and is probably the one you're addressing most. But you've got to be very cautious not to direct all your attention to him or her. If you do, you'll alienate the other people in the room, who probably also have a huge influence on the decision. The best way to manage this situation is to be cautious and include everyone in the room in your conversation. You want to respect them and make them all feel part of the sales process, just as you've done with the whole selling process until now.

Step 3: Determine the Decision-Making Process

To be effective with any group of multiple decisionmakers, it is imperative that you understand the unique decision-making process the group will use—before you begin your presentation. You'll want to tailor your presentation to take that process into account. The easiest way to understand the process is simply to ask how the team will function in its decision making. Of course, there may be more going on than meets the eye, but if you don't think you have

a clear picture, follow up with additional clarification questions until you fully understand their process.

Styles of Leadership

There are any number of leadership and group dynamics that can emerge from this unknown group, so let's look at some of the possible scenarios you're likely to come across.

- *Strong leader with weak followers.* If you convert this strong leader to a champion of your services, you've got the sale made.
- *Strong leader with strong peers.* Make a special effort to take everyone's issues into account. An unconvinced holdout can ruin the deal.
- *Weak leader with weak peers.* Bond with everyone and take the time to educate and move ahead slowly.
- *Weak leader with strong peers.* Make sure you address everyone's questions because the leader will be looking for the others to make his or her decision.
- *Information gatherers for unavailable decisionmakers.* When the decisionmaker is not in the room, you'll have to educate the group on how to sell your product or service.
- *No leader.* Because of the many cross-functional teams that are being formed today to deal with a diverse range of business issues, it is becoming more common to find yourself presenting to an ad hoc committee with no designated leader.

Many of these ad hoc teams have been formed for one particular project and have little organization and no defined decision-making process. This can be a very difficult situation for the unprepared salesperson. When faced with just such an amorphous group, ask outright, "Who's the lead person on this?" If they say, "We're really going to discuss it as a committee and agree together," then ask them to elaborate. "What is your process on this?" Listen for key information in their response. Is the decision actually made by all the people in the room, or is this a committee that's gathering information and then taking it to the real

KEY IDEAS

Teach Client Contacts to Sell Your Idea

Just because you've engineered a meeting with an individual or a group of individuals doesn't mean that all of the decisionmakers are in the room. No matter how careful you are during the precall-planning process, you will sometimes find yourself meeting with someone who reports to a "higher" authority. Even if that's not the case, you need to rehearse the group so they will defend the idea of buying something from you when the competition gets a chance to persuade them otherwise. So start thinking of yourself as a sales coach right from the start. It's your job to teach the prospect how to sell your product or service to someone else.

decisionmaker? Just because it's a group does not necessarily mean that all the decisionmakers are in that room. If they say, "Well, as a committee, we're going to decide," then you just forge ahead. On the other hand, if they say, "Well, this team is going to take our recommendation to Ms. Smith, who really holds the decision power," you'll need to first identify all the issues and challenges and then coach them on selling.

It is important to realize that they're not going to sell your product or service nearly as well as you could. Your job is to coach them on how to sell your product. Perhaps you can hand out a one-page information sheet and then review it: "Most people have found this analysis of our product benefits and cost savings to be really helpful when presenting the pertinent background information to others." What you all usually see is a look of tremendous relief because these people must deliver information, and you have just made their job easier and more organized. Their responsibility is to provide accurate information to the decisionmaker. Your responsibility is to assist them in this effort.

Step 4: Take Control of the Meeting

It is almost impossible to gain the consensus of a group if you don't take control of the agenda. Start by establishing everyone's role, issues, and expectations for the meeting. A clever way to do this is to turn the introduction spotlight on them before the ball gets passed to you. If you've just come in or are completing the review of their decision-making process, you need to take control and say, "Before I start, I'd like to take a minute and, if I could, just hear briefly from each of you what you do and what you'd like to get out of this program." Or if they've already invited you to begin your presentation, you need to say, "I'd be happy to, but before I do that, could I ask, from each of your perspectives, what your objectives are for this program?" Each member of the group will then state his or her agenda. Regardless of the positions they hold—chief financial officer or vice-president of sales—each member has an agenda for the decision. And you need to uncover and understand each one before you start to present your services. Otherwise, you'll be fielding questions from all areas of the company, and the meeting will be out of control. The group's confidence in your presentation will drop accordingly—and your performance will suffer as you find you can no longer relate to the group.

Step 5: Present Your Services

When it's your turn, articulate value by referencing the key bullet points that each person gave you, and describe how your product or service addresses them. Use the information you uncover from the group in the sales presentation. Incorporate it by saying, "George, as you mentioned . . . here's how that would work in the Customer Service Department." Make sure that you include all of the issues mentioned by group members.

Dealing with Questions and Objections from the Group

When someone asks you a question, don't be afraid to ask him to elaborate if you're not clear on what he really wants to know. When you answer, make sure you're concise and very clear about how your product or service can directly answer his concern.

If people are asking questions because they don't understand your product, slow down or back up. Ask them if there's a specific area they'd like more information on. Always take responsibility: "Maybe I wasn't clear on this particular area" or "Let me give you a little more information in that area." Don't make them feel stupid for asking the question.

Conflicting interests is another dynamic that often comes up in groups, particularly with teams that don't get along well. If you've got one person who doesn't want to spend any money, and somebody else who wants to buy whatever you have, then you have conflicting values that must be dealt with: protecting a budget versus delivering some kind of result. Team members should be coming from the same place, but it often doesn't work that way.

When group members start to disagree among themselves, don't take sides. Try to engage those with conflicting points of view in a discussion of priorities so you can understand their different needs. Be a facilitator and flush out all the issues: "From

Selling to a Group

Group dynamics make selling to a group very different from selling to an individual. Keep in mind these three points:

❑ Set the tone of the meeting with introductions to acknowledge all present parties.

❑ Uncover each individual's objectives.

❑ Tailor your presentation to effectively meet the needs of each person in the room.

what I'm hearing, you have concerns with some of the budget constraints. But what I hear over here is that you are responsible for reaching this kind of result. Are there any other concerns?" Get everything out on the table. Then eliminate the arguing and take control of the meeting by answering the issues all at once, rather than one by one.

If you are pulled to either side, or are perceived as taking sides, remember that the one who is hesitating may have just as much influence over the buying decision as the one who wants to go forward. So from a sales perspective, your best position is right in the middle, very convinced and very confident that your product or service is right for them. And then make sure you are including and answering all the objections at once so you can work toward mutual agreement.

Avoid the pitfalls of preconceived notions or assumptions, or of discounting people's input. By addressing all parties in your presentation, you will be best positioned to gain the group's consent and make the sale. If you are to be successful when presenting to multiple decisionmakers, you must stay focused on meeting the individual agendas of everyone present. To be most effective in your sales presentations, never forget that you must win over the members of your audience one at a time.

CHAPTER 16

Become Your Own Sales Manager

Have you ever wondered how sales managers come up with financial goals and help people achieve them? This chapter will explain how it's done. When you're through, you'll be able to set your own goals and manage your time to plan a successful sales campaign. By the end of this chapter, you'll know how to be your own sales manager!

So far we've spent a lot of time talking about the specific details of selling. We've covered learning about your customer's needs and how to work through those needs to arrive at a solution that responds to them. But to be successful at sales, you also need to be aware of the big picture: How not to lose focus while attending to these many details and keep on track with your goal(s).

This is an area where many salespeople slip up. They don't plan for success because "it's too much of a bother" or "it won't work." What these excuses really mean is that they don't want to believe they have control over meeting a sales goal. They don't want to take responsibility for their performance.

What's behind this attitude? The myth of the "natural-born" salesman. Many people aren't aware that they are basing their beliefs and behaviors on a myth. As we've discussed in previous chapters, the natural-born salesman myth says that a salesperson is born, not made. It says that if you are a natural-born salesperson, all you need to do is talk to your prospects, and you'll mesmerize enough of them into signing up to "make things work out okay."

The problem with buying into this myth is just that—you're buying into something that isn't true. Buying into the myth takes control and responsibility for selling away from the salesperson. People who think that selling is part of the genetic package may become filled with self-doubt if they think they don't have the "gene." And those who believe they're "natural-born" salespeople are no better. They often believe that they have "so much talent" they don't need to—or shouldn't have to—work a plan to get clients.

The myth rears its ugly head when it comes to following goals set by management. Perhaps you work for a company that provides you with a strong sales leadership—a sales manager or management team that assists you by setting daily, weekly, and monthly goals; monitoring those goals; evaluating your ability to meet the goals; and designing strategies for improving those goals. It often happens that

in just such a situation, you'll discover a salesperson or two who subscribes to the myth. They are the people grousing about following protocol and meeting the guidelines and standards set by management.

The truth is, these people are operating out of fear, not fact. They don't want to keep track of things, because—buying into the myth—they might find out things are not going as well as they expect them to. They don't want to take responsibility for the fact that they aren't doing what it takes to sell.

No ship would cross the ocean without having a navigator to check readings from navigational aids, to make sure the proper course is being followed, and to make the necessary changes in the ship's direction when it appears the boat is off course. Doesn't it make sense to keep track of your behavior and goals so you can pinpoint trouble spots before they take you off course? Yet "natural-born" salespeople fight this logic with every fiber of their being—and set themselves up for failure.

Well, here's hoping that you are an individual who's willing to do what it takes to become successful at selling. For starters, that means you need to be your own sales manager. It's great if company management provides you with assistance, but no matter how helpful company management is, the responsibility for following a plan still rests on your shoulders.

You have control over what you do. The following five steps show you how to take charge!

Step 1: Analyze the Sales Cycle

To come up with a useful sales campaign, it's important to understand the time frame you're dealing with. So take a clear-eyed view of the sales cycle. How much time will you have to meet your goal? (We'll talk more about how to establish a goal in the next section.)

Depending on your business, you'll find that the basic sales cycle places the most emphasis on daily goals, weekly goals, monthly goals, quarterly goals, and so on. For example, a telemarketer may have to account for daily totals, a magazine salesperson may have to account for monthly totals, and the team at

ATTITUDE ADJUSTMENT

Manage Yourself to the Top

Practice these affirmations.

- ❏ *I am my own sales manager.*
- ❏ *I am doing what it takes to sell.*
- ❏ *I am responsible for reaching my goal.*
- ❏ *I plan to work.*
- ❏ *I work my plan.*

a Fortune 500 corporation, dealing with highly complex projects, may have to account for a sale that spans a year or more.

No matter how long your sales cycle takes, you will eventually need to break the time frame down into smaller, more manageable pieces—in effect, creating the "baby steps" that lead toward your goal.

Here's how to create those "baby steps." Once you've determined *when your actual deadline is*, work backwards. By that I mean, break the larger sales cycle down into smaller, more manageable sales cycles. If your deadlines cover a longer period, you will have to do this several times. For example, if you are concerned about a quarterly report on your sales effort, you will want to break the quarter into months, then weeks, then days.

Once you understand how much time you have, you need to figure out what you need to get done in those periods of time.

Step 2: Set a Base Goal

Before you can assign priorities to each time slot, you need to decide what it is you're trying to accomplish. You need to establish a "base" in terms of dollars. Your goals should be doable and realistic. If you have a sales manager, he or she will probably give you a goal. But if you are on your own, and you have no idea what you should be doing in a certain period of time, you can try to get a sense of what the low, middle, and high performers in your industry achieve in the same time period by calling associations or people in the industry. If you have little or no experience, assume in your first go-around that you're going to try to match the low goals and work your way up from there.

As someone new to selling, your "base" will be the low goal. In selling terms, the "base" is revenue generated from a list of established clients. Most sales teams try to improve on a base. Depending on the economy, the newness of the product, and the degree of competition, for example, the next sales cycle could require a 100-percent or a 10-percent improvement over the previous established base. As a selling newcomer, you have one positive thing to look forward to: Since you're just starting out, chances are you are the most likely person to improve on his or her base, once you get it established!

The dollars brought in by other salespeople in your industry represent not only the amount of gross revenue you'll be generating for the company, but also the amount of money you can plan on earning during your first sales cycle. Most salespeople's income reflects the amount of sales generated. Typically, salespeople earn a commission on what they sell. The commission can vary depending on the industry. In many cases, if you are selling an item costing tens of thousands of dollars, your commission may only be 3 to 6 percent, whereas if you're selling an item that's in the $200 range, your commission may well be more like 15 percent.

Of course, commissions are also determined by other factors such as health care benefits or a base salary. If you're trying to set a sales goal for your own product or company, you'll need to take into account the overall cost to produce and market the product and then tack on the amount of income you need to make. (Keep in mind most business owners don't see any profit or income for quite a few years after starting a business.)

Step 3: Marry Time to Dollars

You know how much time you have to earn a certain amount of money. Now you need to figure out how you're going to do just that, by setting intermediate goals and deadlines.

This is the tricky part. Figuring out what it's going to take to produce a certain dollar goal in a set period depends on a knowledge and understanding of your particular industry, and of yourself. You need to take a look at how much revenue you will typically produce for each sale (i.e., how much does your product cost and how many can you expect to sell in a certain period). Your average sale will probably not reveal itself until you actually start to sell and have a bit of history under your belt. It's a kind of Catch-22 situation.

Still, by working through the information you have at hand, you will be able to come up with a basic plan of attack. Here's an example that may help you work through your own process.

Let's assume that you're starting out in sales, and have few current clients (or none) to service. Most of your time will be spent getting new clients. Later, more of your time will be spent servicing the clients you have. But for now, you need to figure out how many

KEY IDEAS

Checkpoints Keep You from Straying Off Course

Keeping track of your behavior and goals allows you to pinpoint trouble spots before they take you off course.

clients to contact per day. There's probably more than one way to figure this out, but a very elementary way is to start by calculating how much money you would like to make.

Let's say that you want to earn $50,000 a year. The cost of the average item or package you're selling is $1,000. Out of that fee, you earn a commission of 20 percent, or $200. The math is very simple. In order to bring home $50,000 per year, you'll have to sell $250,000 worth of items. That means you'll have to make 250 sales annually, or a sale each business day (assuming two weeks off for vacation and holidays!).

Ask yourself, What is it going to take to make one sale a day? Well, for starters, you're going to have to talk to a number of decisionmakers each day. As we've discussed in previous chapters, you are most likely to close on a sale when you actually meet your buyer face-to-face. So the next logical step is to set up meetings with some of those decisionmakers. Then, most likely, you'll have to make a sales presentation. Since it isn't realistic to expect that everyone you meet or present to will buy your product, you'll need to talk to, meet, and present to more decisionmakers than will actually buy.

If you need to make one sale a day or five sales per week, you know you'll need to get at least five set appointments each week. However, an appointment doesn't guarantee a sale. So you need to plan for more meetings a week than you can possibly close. At some point you'll be able to figure out whether you typically close one in ten, one in five, one in four, or one in three face-to-face sales calls. But for now, you just need to get a plan going. Also, if you've never sold before, you want to take the time to really work with those first few appointments and learn from them, so your ability to close deals will get better as you move along.

For now, you plan on ten face-to-face meetings with customers per week. Now you need to figure out how many calls you need to make to get those meetings set up.

Once again, only time and experience will tell you how many calls you need to make to get a meeting, but for now, a bit of research can help you set initial goals. A trip to the library reveals that there are some very good statistics on how many "dials" per minute and per day an individual is capable of making. You discover it takes an average of six seconds to dial. (Okay, to push the buttons, but you know what I mean!) However, for every dial you make, you'll get a certain number of disconnects, answering machines, or nondecisionmakers.

And, when you do reach a decisionmaker, not every one will agree to a face-to-face meeting. Let's say, one in five decisionmakers will agree to see you. That means, in order to set appointments with ten decisionmakers a week, you need to speak to at least five times as many. In order to speak to fifty (5×10) actual decisionmakers, however, you'll have to make a number of dials per day. Let's say out of every ten dials you make, you get to actually speak to a decisionmaker. That means you'll have to dial the phone five hundred (10×50) times per week, or one hundred dials per day.

Remember, we're talking *dials* here! It only takes six seconds to dial a phone. If all you were doing was dialing, you could reach your quota in a mere fifteen minutes. Naturally, because you have to talk to people at least some of the time, it's going to take a bit longer.

At this point you may be saying, "Gee, that sounds like a lot of work. I want to make a lot more than $50,000, and I don't see how I'm going to if I have to spend all of that time getting appointments."

Well, here's the good news: Remember those financial advisers who try to convince you that it's wise to save, because compound interest can do wonders for pennies socked away in an interest-bearing account? The same is true of sales. You'll always want to work on getting new business to replace clients who drop out and to grow your business beyond your existing base. But repeat business, longer-term contracts, and larger contracts from existing customers will help improve your bottom line dramatically—exponentially, in fact! So will networking and referrals from pleased customers.

But that's in the future. For now, as a new salesperson starting from scratch, your initial goal is simply a place to start. Tell yourself, you can only go up from here!

KEY IDEAS

Plan for More Noes Than Yeses

If you do sell to everyone you present to, you are not presenting to enough people. You should always get some noes. One sales trainer told me that he aims to get one yes out of three calls. That ratio tells him he's doing what he's supposed to be doing—contacting enough people and qualifying them thoroughly before making a presentation. However, depending on the industry, your total contacts may be more or less. So check around. Ask colleagues how their numbers look. Pay special attention to the statistics of top performers.

Step 4: Move from General Goals to Specific Tasks

Now that you've given some thought to the big picture, priorities have started to emerge that will give shape to your days and your week. You know, for example, that the first priority of your day is going to be talking to or meeting with decisionmakers. And, from research, you have discovered the best time to reach those decisionmakers. So anything else you do should be scheduled around that time.

But as a sales professional, you'll be juggling many activities. Some of these activities will put you in direct contact with decisionmakers; other activities are designed to support your effort to be in contact with decisionmakers or to follow through on calls already made. To manage your time in the best way possible, it helps to inventory the activities you'll need to plan for.

Once you have your list assembled, jot down next to each item how much time each activity takes and the best time to do the activity. For example, if decisionmakers in your industry are typically in the office early in the morning and late at night but out during the middle of the day, then that's when you need to try to reach them. On the other hand, if no one in charge arrives before 10:00 A.M., then plan to do other things in the first two hours of your day so you can make the best use of the hours in which you can reach the decisionmakers.

Also note when your personal energy is at its peak. If you are an evening person, you'll want to plan your day the night before, when your brain can still function, and be ready to go—operating on "automatic pilot"—in the morning when your mind isn't fully functional. Of course, if you do your best thinking early in the morning, then you'll want to spend the first few minutes of your day planning and writing proposals and leave the end of the day for less challenging tasks like record keeping.

Depending on your sales cycle, you can spread tasks over a week, two weeks, or a month. For example, a weekly plan might look like this:

Monday:
- ❑ Research and organize leads
- ❑ Plan week
- ❑ Assemble information packets

Tuesday through Thursday:
9:00 to 10:00 A.M.: Organize day
10:00 A.M.: Decisionmakers are in, start dialing!
12:00: Break for lunch. (Note: Two days a week, have lunch with a good networking prospect.)
1:00 to 4:00 P.M.: Call for set appointments

or

10:00 A.M. to 4:00 P.M.: Go out on five set appointments; "cold call" in between
4:00 to 5:00 P.M.: Fill out paperwork, work on sales presentations

Friday:
- ❑ Write follow-up correspondence
- ❑ Mail information packets
- ❑ Write weekly call report and review weekly progress
- ❑ Attend meeting of local business group

Step 5: Total Your Results—in Prospects and in Dollars

You've got the first week planned. Now give it a run-through. As you move through your day, you'll encounter many unexpected experiences. Perhaps on the first call, you will get a decisionmaker who says he's willing to buy without further ado. Or perhaps you'll be told to call back at a later hour; you keep calling back when you're told to, but no one ever comes to the phone! Maybe you set up fewer appointments the first week than you'd planned. Maybe you set up more. Maybe you go out on a set appointment and discover that the person you're meeting isn't really the person you need. Maybe

Repeat Clients Boost Business Exponentially

The need to seek new business never goes away, no matter how long you are in sales. By taking a two-prong approach to selling—building upon an existing base and constantly searching to increase it—you can drive your income up exponentially.

Sales Activities

A sample inventory of sales-related activities might include the following:

❏ Dialing the phone in an attempt to identify and reach decisionmakers

❏ Talking on the phone to actual decisionmakers

❏ Keeping records

❏ Meeting with decisionmakers face-to-face

❏ Follow-throughs: Thanks yous, letter writing, proposal writing, etc.

❏ Promotional activities—mailings, events

❏ Researching prospects or the industry

❏ Planning

❏ Analyzing results and setting new goals

❏ Getting new leads

❏ Servicing current clients

you discover she thought you were from a completely different company, and what you have to sell is completely irrelevant!

Many of these "fiascos" can be avoided by following the information-gathering process. But no matter how hard you try to avoid surprises, you'll always encounter something in the selling process that will astonish you!

Because selling can be so full of surprises and distractions, it's important to stay focused. You need to keep your eyes on the prize, so to speak. And that's where call reports come in.

Call reports, in essence, are exactly what their name suggests: They are reports on the calls you've made. They help you keep track of your progress. They tell you how much you've accomplished each day. They tell you "where to go from here" by enabling you to identify those prospects who are still in the running to buy your product. And they help you guesstimate revenue. At the end of each day, you should always file a call report. (See an example of a call report in the Forms section, in the Appendix.)

In its most basic form, a call report is a sheet of paper listing everyone you've had a meaningful contact with that day (forget about busy signals, hang-ups, etc.). Next to the client's name, write down what you hope to sell them—the item or service, and the quantity. Next write the dollars in revenue the prospect's business represents to you, and assign a percentage that represents the likelihood of the sale occurring. In the next box on the form, note the account status. Finally, the last column represents final results; it's left blank until you have a definite sale (or not).

For example, let's pretend you've identified Company A as a prospect. At this point, you haven't spoken to anyone about actually buying what you have to sell, but you can still enter Company A on your call report. From a fact-finding call, you found out that Company A buys 4 million widgets per year, and each widget costs twenty-five cents. You know there's a possibility that you can be Company A's sole supplier of widgets, because your firm's production can handle producing the number of widgets needed in the time Company A requires. So, after writing 4 million widgets in the service and quantity boxes, you write $1,000,000 in the dollar column of your call report.

Next, you need to assign a percentage representing the likelihood of the client doing business with you. As you become more experienced in your industry, you'll be able to come up with assignment criteria of your own, but for now, we'll use the following model:

100 percent—Sale made; signed contract/bill of sale in hand

90 percent—Say they're going to buy, have had all of the necessary meetings, but no actual signed contract

60 percent—phone calls, meetings with very positive feedback

40 percent—decisionmaker agreed to meet

20 percent—haven't spoken to decisionmaker yet or received a preliminary no

0–19 percent—take them off the list; plan to recontact them in a future sales cycle

Since you haven't spoken to anyone in authority at Company A, you assign the company 20 percent. In the Progress column, you write: "Spoke to assistant in purchasing dept.; call back Tuesday at 10 A.M. to reach Ms. Decisionmaker."

The call report will give you a general idea of how many potential dollars there are out there in your territory and what percentage of them you are likely to get or are actually getting. At the end of each week, review the call reports to see which people on the lists should be carried forward, either because you haven't reached the right person at the company yet or because the prospect is still in the running. The idea is to convert the lower percentages to higher ones as you work through the selling process until they reach 100 percent or you cross them off the list altogether.

Also, look at the amount of revenue that those accounts can potentially generate. As you "work the calls," you'll adjust the potential revenue to come up with more realistic figures. For example, going back to Company A, let's say that by week 2 you've finally talked to

CHECKLIST

Progress Reviews

Daily Progress Review

❑ How many people did you talk to?

❑ How many decisionmakers did you reach?

❑ How many prospects were you able to get appointments with?

❑ What is the average revenue potential looking like?

Weekly/Monthly Progress Review

❑ How am I doing?

❑ Are there any ways to increase efficiency?

❑ Is there any way to work smarter?

❑ What obstacles have presented themselves?

❑ How can I overcome any selling obstacles I'm facing?

❑ Did I commit to my organized plan or allow my personal discipline to slack off?

Exercise:
Write your own weekly and monthly reviews and set goals for the next thirty days.

Call Reports Smooth Out the Ups and Downs of Selling

Using call reports and reviewing your progress keeps you out of trouble. This process forces you to focus on what you're doing—not the crazy ups and downs of the sales game. It helps you understand how much business is out there, how much of that business you can expect to get, and what your progress toward your goal is, so if something isn't working, you can take steps to find a solution.

a decisionmaker. Company A is still in the running because they are looking to buy widgets, but they are looking for a supplemental widget supplier and only need to buy one hundred thousand widgets at this time. Your $1,000,000 sale is now $25,000! Conversely, perhaps they hope to expand and are looking to buy more—in that case, the dollar figure goes up.

Once a client comes through, you can put them on the master revenue list for this particular sales cycle.

Your call reports are essential tools for helping you analyze how well you convert leads to working prospects and prospects to sales. Once you get a sense of how you're doing, you can take a look at what you're doing to see if you can improve your performance.

Step 6: Review the Results

Part of working your regular leads should be a regular review of your sales performance and whether you can improve it. Even though you may not have generated a lot of leads during your first week, it pays to develop good habits early.

So, at the end of each day, review your call report to see where you stand. You need to do the same thing at the end of each week and at the end of each month. During the weekly and monthly reviews, try to get a perspective on your overall behavior and its impact on your long-term strategy.

Step 7: Fine-Tune Your Sales Campaign

As you review your sales methods and techniques, you'll start to figure out what works for you and your clients, and what doesn't. You'll use your periodic review to learn to reach more decision-makers in less time. You'll polish your communication and presentation skills, so you make the sale in less time than you did when you started. You'll become more discriminating and learn to sell larger quantities or bigger packages, so the dollar amount of your average sale will go up.

For instance, perhaps you'll be able to fine-tune your lead lists so you dial more qualified leads to begin with. Maybe by calling receptionists early in the morning, you can qualify the decisionmakers before they arrive at work, so more of the calls spent during the hours decsionmakers are likely to be in will be spent talking to them and not asking preliminary questions of the receptionists. Alternatively, perhaps you'll discover that the decisionmaker is easier to reach at 7:00 P.M. when everyone else has gone home for the day. Then you'll adjust your calling hours accordingly. Perhaps you'll find a way of talking to decisionmakers that works better for you than the method you used when you were just starting out as a salesperson!

Can you become better at scheduling appointments? It makes sense to talk to people who are located in the same area at the same time, so you won't spend a lot of time traveling between meetings. It's much easier to say, "I'm coming down to your area on Thursday of next week to see so-and-so [two businesses located near the client], and I'd like to see you as well. Do you have some time in your calendar to fit me in?"

When you have set appointments in a particular area, schedule them with some "buffer" time, in case an appointment runs over its scheduled time or you get stuck in traffic. But to make the best use of your time, bring along a list of nearby contacts to "cold call" (drop in on without an appointment). Perhaps you'll be able to conduct an impromptu meeting with a decisionmaker. If not, you can use the cold call to jump-start your information-gathering process. Then, when you call the decisionmaker at a later date, you'll no longer be a stranger and can move along the sales process a little more quickly.

It isn't always easy to ride the highs and lows of selling; that's why the next chapter of this book is so very important.

Sales Is a Roller Coaster, but Selling Is a Superhighway

However you arrange your personal selling cycle, don't get discouraged if you have a bad day or even a bad week. Selling is an up-and-down profession. As long as your approach is dedicated, steady, persistent, and consistent, things should even out and you will make your sales goals. It's your job to forge straight ahead!

CHAPTER 17

Becoming a Sales Professional

By now, you've got a basic understanding of how to operate a sales campaign. You know how to:

- Find leads
- Qualify leads
- Gather information about prospects
- Make a sales call
- Handle objections
- Come to agreement and close a deal
- Follow up on sales calls
- Set sales goals
- Manage your time to reach those goals
- Rate your prospects

What's left? Only one of the most—if not the most—important aspects of selling: the *salesperson*.

YOU!

No matter how many books you read or how many sales trainers you meet with, the most important factor in succeeding at sales is the attitude of the salesperson—YOU!

Now, if you've never sold before, that notion can be a bit scary. Our culture depends on commerce to keep it going, but very few people automatically think of sales as a career possibility. Ask a little kid what he or she wants to be, and you'll get police officer, fire fighter, doctor, teacher, maybe even ballet dancer. But, except for a fling with a corner lemonade stand, few children think of sales as a possible career.

As we've discussed, anyone can learn to sell. There are many sales techniques, methods, and approaches that work. Assuming that you're not independently wealthy, at some point in your life you've held a job. Anyone who has ever worked knows that a worker with experience, one who has developed his or her job skills and practiced them regularly, can accomplish a task more quickly and easily than someone with little or no experience performing the same job. With practice, you'll be able to call on the skills we've covered in this book to help you accomplish your goals.

But knowledge, techniques, and skills are useless if you lack the will to apply them. That is why so many of the successful sales seminars out there emphasize self-improvement, "self-actualization," positive thinking, motivational techniques, and a "can do" attitude. Whether it's Anthony Robbins, Dale Carnegie, or Zig Ziglar—they all preach one thing: the importance of your intention. Maybe they try to get you, the salesperson, to see the same thing through somewhat different means, but the message is the same: You have the power to change your life. It's up to you—no one else!

You have the power to succeed at sales! But you need to recognize, process, and deal with any reservations you may have about seeing yourself as a salesperson. If there's any doubt in your mind that you are going to be the greatest salesperson ever, get rid of it now!

Well, you may say, that's easy for you to say. I'm the one out there ready to march into the trenches.

Did I hear you say trenches? That leads me back to my main point: Whatever you think selling is, you're likely to find that it is that way. It's worth spending some time *now* to discover what the blocks to success are that will affect your success *later*.

Selling Is a Growth Process

Selling is a process—of increase and growth. Not just in sales, not just in revenue, but in personal areas as well. The most successful salespeople I've met aren't hucksters. They are well-balanced individuals who truly have their "act" together.

As I said earlier, you don't have to be a sales "know-it-all" to succeed (although by now you certainly know what it takes to succeed in sales). I've met a lot of salespeople, and I have yet to meet one who has claimed to be an instant success! Instead, I constantly meet lots of really successful salespeople who tell me the same thing. They started in the profession knowing nothing, learned their sales methods from watching other experienced, successful salespeople, and achieved success by committing to the process over the long haul.

What made them successful was not what they knew, but how they went about things. Good salespeople share some important characteristics:

- ❑ Enjoys learning about new things
- ❑ Enjoys a challenge
- ❑ Has fun solving problems
- ❑ Has a creative, flexible mind
- ❑ Enjoys meeting new people
- ❑ Sets goals
- ❑ Makes and keeps commitments
- ❑ Finds the "good" in the "bad"
- ❑ Keeps abreast of trends
- ❑ Is a hard worker
- ❑ Builds and maintains relationships
- ❑ Looks for opportunity wherever he or she goes
- ❑ Is organized and a good planner
- ❑ Is enthusiastic about whatever he or she is selling
- ❑ Knows who the competition is—and what they're doing
- ❑ Rolls with the punches
- ❑ Deals with criticism well
- ❑ Has healthy ways to deal with stress
- ❑ Manages time well
- ❑ Knows that he or she is more than his or her job
- ❑ Participates in community affairs and events
- ❑ Is self-reliant
- ❑ Faces obstacles head-on
- ❑ Is responsible and will do what it takes to be a success
- ❑ Enjoys a balanced lifestyle

Far from being a huckster, a successful salesperson is the sort of individual most people would like to be!

If you don't share all of these characteristics, don't worry. *Remember:* A good salesperson likes to learn new things! Part of the fun of being in sales is the self-development process. This self-assessment checklist will help you identify the areas you need to pay more attention to.

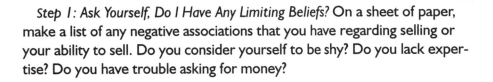

Step 1: Ask Yourself, Do I Have Any Limiting Beliefs? On a sheet of paper, make a list of any negative associations that you have regarding selling or your ability to sell. Do you consider yourself to be shy? Do you lack expertise? Do you have trouble asking for money?

Step 2: Ask Yourself What Is the Positive Aspect of My Negative Belief? Maybe you're thinking, if it's a negative belief, how can there be a positive side to it? Trust me, there always is: A shy person can be better at listening than a person who is outgoing and conversational. A person who lacks expertise is better able to gather information and ask questions than a "know-it-all." A person who has difficulty asking for money is better equipped to enable the buyer to sell himself or herself. Once you start actively looking for the "good" in the "bad," you'll start to understand that very few things in life are all good or all bad! Whenever a negative attitude assaults you, stop and ask yourself what the flip side is! Every cloud has a silver lining, and it's up to you to discover what the silver lining in your particular cloud is!

Step 3: *Focus on Building Up the Positive.* Once you've identified the good qualities you have to offer, focus on them and affirm them. A shy person might say, "I listen well, and I learn a lot about my prospect's needs through listening." If you have an affinity for listening, then work at refining that skill. Build on it to create your unique selling style. It will be a style that works well for you, because a part of you resonates to that particular style. And, once you feel secure in your approach, you'll find it easier to branch out; for example, to become a bit more of a talker, when necessary.

People Skills

- ❏ I am sociable and outgoing.
- ❏ A part of me likes to be the center of attention.
- ❏ I am involved in my local community.
- ❏ I enjoy talking to people.
- ❏ I know how to connect with people.
- ❏ I am good at maintaining relationships.
- ❏ I am a good listener.
- ❏ I enjoy managing people.
- ❏ I can discern other people's needs.

Time Management Skills

- ❏ I am a good organizer.
- ❏ I have established goals.
- ❏ I have a system for selling.
- ❏ I have a plan for promotion.
- ❏ I have all the materials I need to sell and they are readily available to me.
- ❏ My information, leads, contracts, and sales materials are well organized.
- ❏ I manage my time well.
- ❏ I am good at planning my days, weeks, months.
- ❏ My life is balanced between work, family, social, and leisure activities.

Professional Expertise

- ❏ I am an expert in my field.
- ❏ I am excited about what I'm selling.
- ❏ I know who I should be selling to.
- ❏ I know why people should buy my product or service.
- ❏ I read industry publications and attend related events.
- ❏ I know who my competition is.
- ❏ I know what my competition is doing.
- ❏ I know how to network.
- ❏ I know how to work a party.
- ❏ I know how to cold call.
- ❏ I know how to get people to talk to me on the telephone.
- ❏ I know how to work a trade show.
- ❏ I know how to make a presentation.
- ❏ I am good at following through with my contacts.
- ❏ I think creatively.
- ❏ I am good at solving problems.
- ❏ I can see both sides of an issue.
- ❏ I am diplomatic.
- ❏ I am able to foresee objections and to counter them.
- ❏ I want to make money and improve my financial assets.
- ❏ I keep abreast of current affairs.

SELF-ASSESSMENT FOR WOULD-BE SALESPEOPLE

Mental and Physical Health

- ❏ I am self-confident.
- ❏ I have a positive attitude.
- ❏ I believe in myself and my abilities.
- ❏ I have developed healthful ways to handle stress.
- ❏ I can defend myself if someone "attacks" me.
- ❏ I know where my personal boundaries are.
- ❏ I take good care of my health.
- ❏ I spend a reasonable amount of time on my appearance so I look attractive and professional.
- ❏ I always find something positive in every situation, no matter what happens.
- ❏ I exercise regularly.
- ❏ I have a good social support network.
- ❏ I have hobbies and interests outside of my job.
- ❏ I rest and eat well.
- ❏ I have lots of energy.

Ethical-Spiritual Practices

- ❏ I am honest about what I can and cannot do.
- ❏ I never promise what I can't deliver.
- ❏ Bashing the competition is beneath me.
- ❏ I never spread gossip.
- ❏ I don't play "favorites."
- ❏ I sell a good product or service for an honest price.
- ❏ I am worth what I charge.
- ❏ I believe in agreements that serve the best interests of all parties.
- ❏ I follow through on my promises.
- ❏ I am a partner with my client(s).
- ❏ I treat everyone in a company, no matter what office they hold (from janitors to vice-presidents), with courtesy.
- ❏ I never "bad-mouth" people .
- ❏ I focus on the client and the client's needs, rather than on the concerns of my ego.
- ❏ I am successful as long as I do what I say I will do, even if other people don't do what they say they will do.
- ❏ I compete against myself, no one else.
- ❏ I believe in a higher power that ensures things work out for the best.
- ❏ I am a "self-improvement" addict!

So, are you the perfect salesperson? It would be extremely difficult for anyone to be all of these things at all times, but it is a great list to aspire to. And as you do, you are on the road to being the perfect salesperson!

Getting Hooked on Selling

Many people, in fact, get hooked on selling just because the process of learning about themselves and developing into a better person is so much fun. They sell because they get "high" on self-improvement!

This is the *big secret* that hugely successful organizations know. Did you ever wonder why so many people who are apparently successful in other careers get involved in a second business—selling a line of vitamins, proprietary products, or pyramid-like schemes—when it seems to take at least as long for them to make money at building any of these businesses as it would at any other business?

I've known several people who have become involved in a business that involves recruiting other would-be entrepreneurs to establish a network of home-based suppliers of proprietary products ordered from a catalogue. They have yet to retire on the proceeds, yet they stick with it year after year. Why? True, they all profess a respect for the company's products. But there's another, more motivating reason. The one thing they all have in common is the "feel-good" aspect that attending their organization's motivational seminars provides for them. They all understand that it's their positive energy and upbeat attitudes that make them a success. They can't get enough of it!

And neither should you!

Developing a Commitment to Yourself

Successful salespeople have healthy self-esteem. They take responsibility for their actions. They know that it isn't the customer, the product, the company, or the sales manager's responsibility to sell—it's their responsibility. They know they are not perfect, but they don't let their self-imperfections stand in the way of progress. They build their mental, emotional, physical, and psychological fortitude, so that when they have to deal with a difficult personality, a tough problem, or someone who refuses to buy, they can! They have enough self-respect to focus on the good, and get on with their sales campaigns, and their lives.

Now, a whole book could be written—in fact, thousands have been written—on how to stay positive, upbeat, and motivated! How to communicate better, listen more effectively, read body language! How to manage your time! Organize your life! Eat better! Feel well, dress well, and look good!

We don't have enough space here to cover all of the ways you can work on self-improvement—and that's not the issue! What is the issue is getting you to understand the importance of taking care of yourself and how selling can be a force for self-improvement. To paraphrase the inaugural speech of Nelson Mandela (one of my personal favorite motivational aids), there is no point in hiding your light under a bushel. When you shine, you give everyone else around you permission to shine, too! You become inspirational to others. And, as a salesperson, you are in a great position to help other people find good solutions to their problems. You can help them shine!

You can honor this aspect of selling by engineering your own life to help you shine. Try some of the following activities:

- Join or form a support group of positive, proactive people.
- Practice affirmations.
- Schedule "downtime" for rest and renewal.
- Keep a journal of positive actions.
- Make it a habit to read self-improvement books or listen to tapes.
- Read a motivational passage each day.
- Make sure you eat well, exercise moderately, and get enough sleep each night.
- Seek out new opportunities to meet people of principle.
- Challenge yourself to learn new activities.
- Mentally discipline yourself to find the "good" in every situation.
- Commit to principled action.

It may seem at first glance that this list has little to do with selling. It's not a list of techniques or methods, true. But from

Building a Picture of the Ideal

Once again, you can ask questions to help the prospect build a picture of the ideal solution.

Decisionmaker: As I said, we're getting lots of complaints regarding customer service. If it were up to me, I'd hire forty more customer service people.

Software Consultant: What if we could increase the efficiency of your computer system so that fewer people could handle the incoming calls more quickly?

Decisionmaker: How efficient can you make my system?

Software Consultant: What kind of increase in efficiency are you looking for?

another point of view, it is far more important than any technique or method we've covered, because it focuses on you—the salesperson. If you do the things on this list (or a few others you may think of on your own), you'll find vast reserves of energy you never knew you had before. You'll be less stressed because you'll have engineered your own means of support. You'll know that you are a person outside of whether an individual says no or yes at the end of your sales call. You'll have the equanimity to handle the tough customer, to continue to keep in touch with the prospect who says no to what you have to offer, and to give that person the opportunity to say yes at a later date! And, believe me, many of them will say yes later, if you continue to do all of the things we've already discussed. You'll find that your achievements will be greater all the way around, because you are focusing on what you're doing, and not on what everyone else is doing, not doing, or has to say.

You are on your way to realizing the secret attraction of sales—there is nothing more exciting than selling, because there is nothing more exciting than embarking on a plan for personal growth!

I know you're going to shine!

CHAPTER 18

Building Sales Through Electronic Media

The Internet is regarded by many as the sales tool of the future. It enables businesses to reach customers who wish to buy anything at any time, day or night and who live anywhere in the world. Although Internet sales are still in their infancy, they have tremendous potential. Many business ventures are banking on building sales to phenomenal proportions via the Internet. In fact, rumors are circulating that salespeople in some industries soon may be outmoded due to electronic sales.

On the other hand, successful salespeople have always maintained that it's the personal connection with the client that leads to success in sales. If that's the case, it may indeed be premature to assume that the convenience and ease of buying goods via the Internet will pull all business away from the traditional salesperson.

What is more certain is the positive impact electronic media can have on any sales effort. The Internet offers limitless amounts of information including leads; access to industry research; a speedy means of communication to clients via e-mail; and easy access to motivational materials and self-development tools, all at the click of a button. The Internet enhances the traditional salesperson's connection with the client because it enables the salesperson to better service the client by forwarding white papers, reports, proposals, communiqués, memos, and research to the client. In addition, your own Web site can pull qualified customers directly to you. There are numerous ways a Web site can be used to augment your sales efforts or to generate qualified leads—and it's at work twenty-four hours a day, seven days a week.

You simply can't afford to be in sales today and not be using electronic media to support your sales effort! Ironically, considering how little it costs to buy a "place" for yourself on the world wide Web, today's businesses are not perceived as stable and professional unless they have a Web address in their literature. Having a Web site builds consumer confidence, and in the case of a salesperson, client confidence.

A well-designed Web site also can cut the costs of the sales effort. Catalog and postage expenses decrease as people are able to immediately print out any product sell sheet or other business information of interest. You may be able to cut back on local paper and trade advertising expenses, which can add up quickly for a small business. With a Web site you no longer have to cover as much information in your ads—you can use them to send traffic to your Web site, instead. By prequalifying leads over the Net, you can identify customers who are more likely to be seriously interested in what you have to sell.

The Basics of Internet Use

There are many books on the market today geared toward helping the novice understand the Internet, including its usefulness as a marketing tool. Recent publications have even started to take a look at successful Web page design—something of a new specialty in the field of graphic art. We won't be able to cover everything about sales and marketing on the Internet in this book, but this chapter will at least cover some important basics about the Web. Think of it as a crash course, a sort of *Cliff Notes* on Web-based marketing, and plan to spend some time later checking out the many resources that exist and delving more deeply into the marketing topics that interest you.

The biggest expense connecting to the Net is, of course, buying a PC, palmtop, or laptop computer. However, computer costs have been dropping dramatically, and the forecast is that they will become even more reasonable in the future. Key items in purchasing a computer for Internet use are memory (Internet sites are becoming more graphic, and graphics take a lot of memory); modem speed (56 K is the new standard); and whether it comes pre-loaded with Internet browser software.

Most computers sold today are Internet ready; that is, they are already loaded with a browser, such as Netscape™ Navigator or Microsoft's™ Internet Explorer. Using a browser is simply a matter of entering the Internet site address, commonly called the URL (Universal Resource Locator), and typically within seconds the home page you want to access will be up on your screen.

Gathering Information via the Internet

As a sales and/or marketing person, you no doubt will choose to spend some time searching out information on specific accounts,

industry and trade organizations, government regulations, and related news events. You may want to join a list service, which will e-mail you topic updates periodically, or join a chat group for ongoing industry-related discussions.

If you don't have a specific site to look up, but you want information about a subject, then you can use one of the many excellent search engines to assist you in your quest. Alta Vista™, Yahoo™, InfoSeek™, and Lycos™ are some of the more popular search engines out there. There are minor differences between these engines. One may be well known for word search capabilities, for example, while another is more geared toward a business search index. However, the good news is that once you have searched on one engine, you can always conduct a search on another if you are dissatisfied with the first search results.

The Dangers of Irresponsible Internet Use

A caveat: Using the Internet may be speedier than getting into your car, driving to and from the library, and conducting your own search with the aid of a reference librarian, but it still takes time. Many people do not realize just how much time searching the Internet can take. If you don't know the exact location of the information you're requesting—that is, if you don't have a specific Web site address—you can spend a lot of time checking out sites returned by search engines only to find they don't meet your needs.

The Internet environment can be very distracting. Ads, animated graphics, news blurbs, and more can easily distract you from your task at hand. Often, the thought of searching for a bit of information on an item of personal interest pops into a user's head at an inopportune moment, tempting even a serious business person to "surf the Net" to resolve the question. Before she knows it, she's wasted an hour or more of time that would have been better spent on selling.

Using the Internet also can be quite addictive, as psychologists have noted more than once in the contemporary press. So don't let yourself go—at least, not while on your business/company time. Schedule an Internet fun and games night once a week, and stay organized and efficient during working hours.

Finally, there is the danger of downloading information from the Internet that you think is fact, but which, in reality, may be false. Many sites on the Net are constructed by amateurs or by companies seeking to promote themselves. There is no independent monitoring or fact-checking organization making sure that what you find on the Net is accurate. One assumes that conventional newspapers and magazines who have had a long history of fact-checking and ethical policies in reporting the news will bring the same editorial approach to their online publications, but that is not always the case. It's extremely important to view any information you find on the Web with a critical eye.

The Cost of Hooking Up— and How to Do It

Over and above the cost of a modem, the average Internet service is between $15 and $30 per month, and typically includes up to 10 megabytes of space to support a modest Web site.

You can find an Internet service provider by checking out www.webweek.com, the Web site for Internet technology. The same site will enable you to familiarize yourself with the Internet and issues related to it, including news about technical advances and tips for using it strategically.

Choosing a Name for Your Web Site

Once you have a provider, you'll need to choose a name for your Web site. Make it easy for your customers. If your business is called Great Shoes, then www.greatshoes.com would be an easy-to-remember name/Internet address for your customers. As with anything else, you don't want to make your clients think too hard!

It is probably best that you purchase a domain of your own, rather than purchase a Web page as a sub page of your Internet service provider's directory or some other site's directory. If you do not, your customers will have to type in a "path" to locate your Web site. Having to type a path makes typos more probable and locating your information more difficult.

KEY IDEAS

Web Site Strategy

Setting a strategy for your Web site is the first step to success. A great strategy should succinctly outline the results you want your Web site to achieve. Do you want to increase your sales? Generate more good quality leads of people who use your products? Have a certain percentage of your sales come from E-Commerce? It is important that your strategy clearly define what your goals are and how you plan on achieving them.

Once you decide on a possible name for your Web site, you'll need to do a search to make sure no one else has that domain name already. For starters, you can type it in the address bar of your Internet service provide: www.[yournamechoice].com, and see if the ISP pulls it up. If not, chances are no one else is currently using that name.

To increase the likelihood that the domain name is available, further checking is necessary. Call up www.register.com and follow the instructions on this Web site to search for your preferred domain name. This site also connects you with an optional trademark search engine. These services aren't free, but the fees they charge are modest and well worth it if they serve to help avoid conflicts over name rights in the future.

Creating a Web Page

Once you have your domain name registered, it's time to create a Web page. Your ISP no doubt will offer hints, tips, suggestions—many even offer tutorials—for creating a Web page of your own. If you still feel a bit intimidated about creating a Web page by yourself, consider taking a class in the subject. Chances are your local community college offers a variety of courses in Web design. Look for courses that will enable you to become knowledgeable enough to use a Web page editor—that is, a program that enables you to create a Web page without having to write code. Two popular Web page editors are FrontPage and Adobe PageMill. (See Appendix F for more information on Web-based learning tutorials, as well as a list of Internet sites with content that salespeople may find useful.)

Learning to use a Web page editor will take time, however, so don't fool yourself into thinking that putting up a page will happen overnight. If you don't have the time to devote to learning a new program (the Web page editor), then you'll want to call on the talents of a professional designer—a Web master. Some Internet service providers offer the service for free or for a modest fee, as a bonus for signing on. You also can look in your local Yellow Pages for Web designers.

Web Site Design Tips

1. Create Immediate Visual Interest

To avoid putting people to sleep when they visit your site, avoid long text blocks, large charts, and long lists. Keep in mind that most computer screens offer less usable space than an 8 1/2 × 11-inch sheet of paper turned sideways. And that often the browser box isn't open to the full size of the screen.

It's probably best, therefore, to start with a short paragraph that comes directly to the point. Eye-catching graphics—possibly your company's logo used in a creative way—are a plus, although it's important not to use too large a picture file; otherwise, it will take a long time for the page to download, and customers may become irritated or impatient at the wait.

A directory of links to other sections of your Web page, or other pages in your site, should be positioned along the left-hand side of the page—the side that's most likely to be seen when the browser window isn't open to its fullest. The directory of links acts like a contents page to your site, but differs from a conventional contents page in that the headings listed should be limited to one word or a very short phrase.

Color can help spruce up even a very simple site. Make sure, though, that the colors you choose for your site reflect the tone of your industry; for example, while primary colors seem to suit a site selling children's toys, they might not inspire the sense of stability and seriousness bank customers are looking for. If you can, incorporate the same color you're using on your business cards, stationery, and other promotional literature. This will help build a consistent image. A caveat about color: All colors don't look the same on every browser, so make sure you view your design in both Netscape™ Navigator and Microsoft's™ Internet Explorer before finalizing your design.

Choose type that is bold and clean. Fancy types do not read well on a computer screen; resolutions on a monitor are not as clear as that on a printed sheet of paper, and you may find it necessary to use a large type size throughout (12 points and above), to make copy easy to read.

KEY IDEAS

Web Site Goals

Goals for a Web site usually comprise two parts, one very tangible and the other intangible. For example: The site will increase revenue and improve customer loyalty by learning about customers needs and offering them customized products and solutions they can order quickly and easily.

The results of Web page goals are measured by a target audience. How is the Web site going to make that target audience feel? What is the Web site going to make the target audience do?

2. Give Visitors a Reason to Come Back

Format your Web site so that people will revisit it often. Incorporate new product launches, upcoming trade shows and times, promotional events, links to other Web sites of interest to your clients, research papers, press releases, and questions and answers.

3. Enable Visitors to Contact You via the Site

If someone has made the effort to look you up on the Web, chances are they're interested in learning more about what you have to offer, or possibly even in ordering something directly from your site. A "request for information form" is a good way to register potential leads; it should ask for the name, address, phone number, and e-mail address of guests to the site. As a means of encouraging registration, offer those who registered an e-mail newsletter, a catalog, or product samples.

A request for information form is a good start, but there are many other ways to service customers through your Web site. An online catalog can be a helpful tool for boosting sales. It may be a simple price list together with an e-mail order form, or it could be a more elaborate chart or even a catalog with pictures.

4. Create Some Fun

Jokes, cartoons, contests, trivia, frivolous questions, or prizes awarded to every hundredth visitor to the site will help bring visitors back again and again.

5. Update Your Site Frequently

Nothing is older than yesterday's news. Keep your site current, or people will not be interested in coming back. It's not unusual to find sites on the Web that haven't been updated in a couple of years or which have been abandoned altogether. Such sites do not convey a professional image! If your site becomes too cumbersome to update, then change it so it's simpler and perhaps doesn't require much updating.

6. Register the Site with Major Search Engines

All major search engines offer you the ability to register your site address. Make sure you use key words that summarize what you have to sell when you register the site; these key words are key to the engine pulling up your URL address when people specify the same words in their searches.

7. Cross-Market Your URL Address

If people don't know about your Web site, it won't do you much good—no matter how fancy it looks or how complete the information on it is. Beyond the occasional visitor who finds you randomly in a topic search, there are many other clients who would visit your site if only they knew it existed. Visitors may be motivated to visit a Web site when they want to avoid a sales presentation and yet find out what you have to offer. So make sure you put your Web address on all sales literature so that they can discover the useful features of your site. If they do register via the "request for information form," you can follow up with a phone call or letter later.

8. Build an Image

Don't just use your Web site for obvious advertising and cataloging. Insert a list of frequently asked questions (FAQs) or include some broad applications information that is aimed at building your image as a knowledgeable source. This gives you a positive image and motivates the visitor to bookmark your address for future visits when similar needs arise.

Using E-Mail

Few things irritate people more than SPAM—unrequested e-mail sounding too good to be true and promising dubious get-rich-quick schemes. But following up instantly on meetings, phone calls, or other communications with a client are another story. Customers appreciate a brief, follow-up note, to-the-point action list, or thank you letter. Nothing beats the speed and efficiency of a prompt e-mail response.

For the small business, e-mail can constitute a significant cost savings over the telephone and mail service. After the monthly user fee, there is no cost for e-mail. Sending letters at no cost feels great and encourages you to be even better at following-up with potential customers.

KEY IDEAS

Use E-Mail for Sales Follow-Up

Research has shown that 70 percent of all sales are made after the fifth contact. However, most salespeople stop selling efforts after the second contact. See the problem? Just when the customer is beginning to warm up, most sales follow-up has been tossed aside. Obviously you are missing sales opportunities, but even more so, you aren't getting paid appropriately for the time you have invested! Don't let go of a prospective customer until you both decide it's not a good fit!

Generating Qualified Leads

If you've done a good job of developing an interesting Web site, chances are that many of the people who have made the effort to seek out your site are going to sign up for more information.

Offering an online questionnaire for visitors to fill out, the aforementioned request for information form, is one way for you to qualify leads. By designing a questionnaire that requests considerable background material and an explanation of the customer's needs and problems, you'll have gone a long way toward qualifying the Internet lead.

If they fill it out!

My experience with the Internet is that people who use it have a very short attention span. People often use the Internet to avoid a sales call, maintain anonymity or privacy, and/or because they are too impatient to obtain information through slower means, like snail mail. I'm not aware of any studies on the best way to design an Internet questionnaire, but I do have a few suggestions for points to consider:

- Carefully assess the minimum amount of information you need to get from the visitor. What is the amount below which any response from the form will be useless? Is it their name and address? Then make those items required. Don't allow anyone to send you a form that doesn't have those two items completed—otherwise you'll waste your time downloading and inspecting the response.
- Other items can be optional. But just as with a snail-mailed survey, make the rest of the survey questions easy to read and, whenever possible, fun to answer.
- Try to limit the length of the questionnaire to one or one-and-a-half screen lengths. People simply may not bother to take the time to scroll further.
- Make the submit button obvious by labeling it submit or send. Make it relatively big, and put it in a spot that the eye is likely to hit. (The submit button is the one visitors to your site will click to e-mail the form to you.)

- Offer a reward for completing the questionnaire! The "reward" can be a printed catalog of the products you wish to sell, free product samples, or a free consultation. Make sure to check out legal issues if you decide to run a contest. Some states prohibit sweepstakes, etc. and, since people from around the world will have access to your site, you'll need a legal disclaimer regarding entries submitted from states and countries that have laws about such things. A good attorney will have to be consulted if you wish to get involved in something that complicated.)

Once you get a response from your Internet information form, your response to this qualified lead should be to contact the potential customer to gather more information. If you don't want to scare this lead away, you'll need to employ the same customer-focus approach described elsewhere in this book and keep the relationship at the information-gathering stage while you build a relationship.

Direct Mail Electronic Style

If you've been collecting e-mail addresses with your information requests, then you'll want to treat them like the valuable commodity they are and use them judiciously for sending out product announcements, news releases, or even newsletters.

Whichever purpose you choose, don't put all of the relevant information in the communication. Keep back the more in-depth details, which will require them to return to your Web site or to contact you for more information. Announce that new product, but require them to come to your site for exact product specifications. Announce the lead to a story, but get them back to read the full article.

As with phone and fax soliciting, you may also find that there are unique e-mail address lists you'll want to purchase. If they're the right lists for you, this may be a very cost-effective approach, as the traditional printing and mailing costs don't exist. However, as with any other kind of direct mail, many people automatically trash unsolicited e-mail, so you'll need to first test the medium as to the list's effectiveness.

KEY IDEAS

Mistaking Busy for Producing Leads

When you are busy all day long, it feels great! However, at the end of your day it doesn't matter what you did, it matters if you did the right things! Don't mistake busy for productive. Don't hope for the sales to happen; make them happen. Don't be reactive; be proactive. Real productivity comes from a well-designed strategy of generating leads and following up on a day-to-day basis.

Web Site Drawbacks

Expect your competition to visit your Web site when they learn that you have one. Be sure to keep this in mind when you're developing content for your business Web pages.

Don't give away proprietary tricks or services; make sure your content provides more of a general service. Save the unique extras and special services for sales-closing sweeteners.

For those who do request additional information, make sure you send it out promptly. Remember, all Web sites require constant attention and upkeep. Not only is there the pressure of constant incoming e-mail, but, as we've noted before, the site should be updated at a minimum of every two weeks. It is very easy to let this updating slip, but don't. Anyone visiting your pages frequently will notice this immediately. Attention to such details sends a subtle message to your customer base about the qualify and execution of your work.

The Web in Your Future

There comes a point with any new technology when you have to get on board or risk missing the boat entirely.

Anyone who held back too long in becoming familiar with the PC for everyday business use likely came to the point where they had to scramble to catch up, and they felt somewhat overwhelmed at the prospect. The general usage and applications that rapidly followed the introduction of the personal computer gave early users a competitive edge.

Today, use of the Internet is much the same case. Its power as a communicator is only now being discovered and developed. The use of its information-gathering power is just now being understood and applied in business. Sales of products over the Net have jumped drastically in just the past couple of years. Net business applications will undoubtedly increase exponentially for years to come.

If you're not using the Internet now to support your sales efforts, you need to get started. Don't wait until doing business on the Web becomes a necessity. With the cost of admission so low, get in early on the learning curve and find out for yourself how best to use the Internet to build your business leads and sales.

Keep focused on reaching and servicing customers. And send them the message that your business offers the latest in products and services and is a business on the cutting edge.

CHAPTER 19

Hitting the Road

Why set goals? Sales success is not an accident. Those sales-people who achieve the most in their careers generally have one thing in common: They know where they are going and exactly how they are going to get there.

Goal setting is the process you use to accomplish this. Why do you need to set goals? The answer is really very simple. Setting goals is the most efficient way to accomplish your objectives. It works in a number of ways.

Goal setting achieves the following:

- It directs and coordinates your activities.
- It increases efficiency through prioritizing.
- It keeps you motivated.
- Most importantly, it is the way you steer your ship.

What good is making efficient use of your time without ensuring that you're headed in the right direction? When properly used, goal setting should be the rudder that directs and coordinates your business activities. It keeps you focused on what's important, and on what's necessary to grow to the next level of success.

Goal Setting Increases Efficiency Through Prioritizing

Goal setting focuses and prioritizes your activities so the bulk of your energy goes into accomplishing those objectives that are key to achieving your major goals. It avoids the trap of keeping too many balls in the air, and it emphasizes those two or three key activities that are really critical to bigger successes. Rather than wasting your time trying to accomplish everything in your workday, it helps you sort through those "must do" activities from those "like to do" ones that can eat up your precious time and dramatically slow you down.

Goal Setting Keeps You Motivated

Establishing goals that are meaningful and personally challenging is a good way to keep yourself motivated and interested in the progress of your business activities. Imagine your work without any goals. Can you just see yourself toiling away endlessly to do better and better, with no

real sense of progress? Goal setting turns this around by defining significant steps you focus on in your quest for larger, broader goals. It gives you a sense of accomplishment as interim objectives are achieved, and it provides a way for you to take pride in the recognition of your progress.

Plan for Success

One of the most important aspects of goal setting is that it helps you visualize exactly what success means to you.

The process of establishing goals demands that you review all the business and personal options open to you. From these options, you must then select the goals that are most important—by your definition, and by your analysis of your business objectives. These goals, when achieved over long periods of time, will give you a sense of excitement and enthusiasm as they are planned for, methodically worked toward, and hopefully achieved after significant hard work.

Goal setting is a way for you to define success on your own terms. It gives you a framework from which to look at the various aspects of your work and life, and then it allows you to assign priorities and objectives to these so you can develop a sense of control over your future.

Define Your Business by Defining Your Goals

The process of defining your business goals really defines the actual business you're in. After you've set down those goals that are key to your success and growth, what you've really done is defined those guidelines that are going to regulate your day-to-day activities and control how, and on what, you spend your workday.

That's why setting goals is so key, for how well you define your goals determines how well your time will be spent in your daily activities. You can easily spend your days caught in the frenzied pace of uncoordinated, hectic activities that lead nowhere, or you can grab the bull by the horns and establish a disciplined effort to build your sales and your career.

Becoming Complacent

When you've been in sales a long time, there's two things to watch for.

You plateau because you're successful and happy, and you're having a great life. The problem is that you really can't stop in selling. You're either going forward or you're going backward.

You get overconfident, which is again discounting all the things you did right in the beginning.

Many times I've heard people say, "I used to do this and it worked." Ask yourself, "When did I stop doing this?" Many times all you may need to do is rebuild the good skills and discipline you once had.

Setting Goals Avoids Sales Plateauing

As your sales successes grow over time, you can approach the point where you keep tremendously busy but make no more headway in increasing your sales productivity. Whatever objectives you have set for yourself, you can reach a point of comfortable sales activity at which it appears you can continue indefinitely. You're making a good living, and without any unforeseen problems arising, why change things?

Sounds good, but this kind of thinking is dangerous.

It's hard to stay motivated and at the peak of your game if each day feels like a repeat of the last. By keeping aggressive plans and objectives, you are able to keep that "carrot" of sales growth in front of you. By having an eye on the future, you are better able to fight through the morass of those hectic daily activities that can easily swamp you. And it's far easier to stay enthused if you perceive your activities as means to an end rather than ongoing tasks with no objectives.

If you find your attitude or your sales slumping, perhaps it's a good time to review your goals to make sure you're still imposing a sense of urgency about your business. Being successful in sales has a lot to do with keeping aggressive goals for yourself, and enjoying the accomplishment of those goals by having a good attitude and a realistic plan for accomplishing them.

For similar reasons, goal setting avoids stagnation in your business. It's important to cultivate a healthy attitude toward continually improving your sales and business targets. By placing pressure on yourself to do better each successive period, you automatically are forced to review your past activities to look for more productive approaches. Also, you develop the orientation of continuously looking for personal and business efficiency improvements, which means that you never end up resting on your past accomplishments. This constant focus on business growth and improvement avoids much of the stagnation that can follow when one becomes too complacent with past performance. Active goal setting breaks down the lulling effect of "business as usual."

Goal setting is also an excellent technique to promote business growth. Beyond providing personal motivation and avoiding a sense of stagnation, the process of defining your goals yields the means through which you actually grow, and direct, your business. For example, seeking to get sales from some new market segment may not only bring you those additional sales, it also may position your business in a particularly attractive growth market, which may be critical to its long-term survival.

Goal Setting Keeps Activities in Balance

Goal setting is a process that defines objectives in the various activities that compete for your time and attention. Used in conjunction with a systematic time management plan, it is a way to balance your efforts so you don't focus on one or two objectives to the exclusion of others. By tracking your progress toward these goals, you ensure that objectives of equal importance receive similar attention and efforts. When you don't take the time to manage your time and goals, you lose your perspective of what's important to your business, and focus more on what you like to do. Be aware of how much you gain in efficiency and control by utilizing a strong goal-setting approach in your daily, monthly, and yearly planning.

Where Should You Set Goals?

Goal setting should not be restricted to your business efforts only. Of course, it makes sense to plan your sales activities with major accounts or for key industry objectives. Certainly you can apply this same discipline more broadly to your business as you build, from a focus on individual accounts, to include major programs that address significant business activities.

Expand the application of goal setting and planning further to include your personal life, family and friends. Many people overlook the importance of planning for their personal life as well as for their business activities. Don't write this area off. It's equally important to your overall mental health, and if you're not making the effort to enjoy and reward yourself, then maybe you've forgotten the whole point of working so hard in the first place.

If it's a goal that's important to you, plan for its success by focusing on the individual steps that will eventually lead to even more accomplishments and satisfaction. Follow the old adage, "Work hard, play hard." Perhaps rewrite it, "Plan your work, plan your play," and you'll find time for both and enjoy success with both.

The Process of Goal Setting

- Put your goals in writing.
- Make your goals personally challenging.
- Actively pursue your goals.
- Reward yourself when you succeed.
- Update your goals periodically.

Failure to Do Adequate Precall Planning

Being poorly prepared is the number one reason why sales people don't get the sale.

Your competition outsells you because they know more about the client situation than you do, and they do a better job. If you've developed the right relationship along the sale, then sometimes you can have a conversation with the buyer and ask, "What have I done wrong?" And they might tell you outright, "You messed up. If you do X, Y, and Z, then you're still in the running."

Put Your Goals in Writing

If it's important enough to spend this amount of time and effort figuring out what you want to accomplish, then it's important enough to put it in writing. Take out three pieces of paper. Label the first, "Account Goals"; label the second, "Business Goals"; and label the third, "Personal—Self, Family, and Friends." Then take the time to *define what's both important and critical for you* in each of these areas.

Be specific in your goals. Quantify them to the best extent possible. Rather than saying, "I want to greatly increase my sales next year," state specifically, "I want to achieve sales growth of $300,000 next year." Instead of planning on spending more quality time with your family, define the number and length of vacations you are going to take with them over the next year, and even the number of hours you are planning to spend in play activities with your kids each weekend.

Commit yourself in writing to your goals. Put them on the bulletin board over your desk so you can continually remind yourself what you should be focused on.

Make Your Goals Personally Challenging

Don't define mediocrity with your goals. Make them significant and worthy of your best efforts. How can anyone be expected to get excited and motivated over goals that require no straining or heavy lifting? Remember, these goals are for yourself. Make them a stretch. Make them difficult and large enough so you get excited just at the thought of accomplishing them.

Alternatively, as challenging as they should be, they should not be unattainable. If they're almost out of the question, how can you ever be expected to commit to them wholeheartedly?

Then get a second opinion wherever possible. Test these goals on your peers, your accountant, your family, on whomever it may be appropriate. If they say, "So what?" crank them up a notch. If they give a little smile or a low whistle, you know they're just right.

Actively Pursue Your Goals

If you've taken the time to establish meaningful and challenging goals for yourself and your business activities, then fully committing to them should be your endorsement that they are truly important to you. If you just give lip service to this activity, don't expect too much. Maybe

you'll knock off a couple of the easier items, but what the heck, who has time for all this stuff anyway?

Take the time, make the effort, or stop kidding yourself. Life—and your workday—are too short to waste giving token attention to an activity as important as this. Commitment to your goals should be your highest priority. Work like a demon, believe you're going to succeed, and you will. You'll find yourself fully absorbed and having fun in the process. Remember, you can achieve only what you believe you can achieve. Set your goals high, be tenacious, and expect to win. You will!

Reward Yourself When You Succeed

What's the fun of working so hard if you don't take the time to enjoy your accomplishments? Feeling good about yourself is half the battle, anyway. And as important, since these are valid and challenging goals, realize these really are significant accomplishments and that you deserve credit for them.

Acknowledge your successful efforts, and help keep your spirits up by rewarding yourself whenever you have a chance to cross off one of the items on your goal lists. It's not that often that you'll get the chance to acknowledge your successes. Take the time to pat yourself on the back and spoil yourself a little.

Again, the whole point of your work is to enjoy your successes on both business and personal fronts. Do something special to celebrate. Perhaps a long-promised fishing trip, perhaps even trading in the car for an upgrade. Take the time to recognize and celebrate your successes and you'll stay motivated toward even greater achievements.

Update Your Goals Periodically

As you find yourself making periodic progress toward your goals, make sure you modify or add others to reflect this. Although the goals should be personally challenging and significant, you will find that by breaking them down into smaller time frames, monthly or weekly, they become more manageable.

You will also find that your short-term goals will have to be amended more often than your longer-range goals. Although the long-term objectives for yourself and your business tend to change slowly, the methods and opportunities to implement many of the building-block activities will change in response to numerous factors. You will find it vital to review

Nervousness

It is normal to expect that at times, particularly when you are starting out in sales, you will find yourself quite nervous over an upcoming sales call.

At times like this, you should shift your thoughts away from the customer and focus on thinking about your strengths and what you bring to the table. With all your preparation and product knowledge, shift your focus to the other person and think about why they want to hear from you.

This shifting of focus and not worrying will naturally relax you, and you will find it much easier to be genuinely sincere and also easier to project enthusiasm and confidence in your presentation.

your goals quite regularly in response to competition, other opportunities, or even a family illness.

Planners Win!

People who plan their daily activities have a competitive advantage over those who don't. Defining your goals and developing a time management system to accomplish them is the best way to succeed in your business.

For you, and for your business success, attainment of these goals is recognition of your commitment to the quality and high performance of your personal business efforts. Sales can be a very lone effort, and likely you receive little attention for your daily routine. Of course, everyone likes to look at their sales tally at the end of the month or quarter, but that speaks little about all of the other activities you must address throughout the same period. Don't let all the other sales development and support efforts slip from your attention. Recognize, through your goal achievement, that they are also important parts of your work.

Besides giving you a sense of progress, the setting of goals and their periodic attainment is a good mechanism to keep you feeling positive about your work. If you limit all your positive feedback simply to your bottom-line sales, then you are measuring only one dimension of your progress and performance.

Additionally, such a singular measure may keep you overly focused on the sales numbers not focused enough on the balance of your business activities. Over the long term, your sales success will come from having a system that defines and controls your efforts over the broad range of your total business activities.

Goal setting should be the foundation of your business.

By setting goals that are meaningful, being fully committed to their attainment, and tracking your progress against them, you can develop a powerful formula for sales success.

Epilogue

Lastly, let's talk about the culture of sales.

Every profession has a culture of its own, and sales is no exception. In fact, the selling profession can be seen as having two cultures: One that has been manufactured for it by novelists, moviemakers, and other contributors to popular culture; the second that is constantly being cocreated by ambitious, optimistic salespeople and their mentors.

In the first category, the picture we get of selling is less than admirable. Thanks to a number of mid-twentieth-century American novelists, moviemakers, and, most notably, playwright Arthur Miller, author of the 1949 Pulitzer Prize winning play *Death of a Salesman*, selling as a profession has had a dubious place in American culture. Although America's booming capitalist economy and entrepreneurial success stories could not have been possible without salespeople, popular culture depicts the salesperson as pathetic, a "loser," classless, and ethically and morally inferior. The person is seen as either being unable to control his or her own destiny or as a shark who tears everyone else to pieces to achieve greedy ends (as in the movie, *Glengarry Glen Ross*).

It is important to look at the effects that the "culture" of sales has on members of the profession, because, if we are constantly surrounded by an environment based on certain ideals, images, and models of behavior, we will inevitably be influenced by the messages of that culture. Even if we see ourselves as strong, independent-minded individuals who can "fight" negative influences, we will still be wasting a lot of energy doing the fighting, so to speak. As a salesperson, therefore, it is important to engineer your environment so that you can recognize and address the negative images in our culture towards salespeople and instead surround yourself with positive, proactive images. If you are not conscious of the negativity that exists in society towards a sales effort, you may sometimes feel a nagging unease about what you're doing that may help to undermine you. Of, you may decide not to try for a rewarding career in sales, because you don't know where to look for more positive images.

A charming movie by Whit Stillman, *Barcelona*, offers a commentary on the salesman mystique. The main character, Ted Boynton, played in the movie by Taylor Nichols, summarizes how he fell in love with the sales profession. In a monologue in the movie, Boynton recalls how, "Like nearly everyone else, I had seen Arthur Miller's play, and as a youth had the usual sneering and deprecating attitude to the world of business and sales . . . all that changed senior year when the charismatic Professor Woodward Thompson's business course convinced us that even the apparently mundane world of business had its romance . . . ." He goes on to say how, in sales, he found "not just a job, but a culture. Franklin, Emerson, and Carnegie and Bettger were our philosophers, and thanks to the genius of Carnegie's theory of human relations, many customers also became friends . . . ."

In Boynton's sales model, "high pressure" sales—the kind of sales mocked by popular culture—doesn't really have anything to do with selling, but is instead a form of fraud. In true sales, he says, "you're providing a real and constructive service, helping people make their lives more agreeable or their companies more efficient, and in so doing creating wonderful economies of scale from which everyone and the whole economy benefits."

In this model, selling is a way for almost anybody to raise himself or herself from failure to success, as Boynton's hero, Frank Bettger, the author of a book on the subject, alludes. "The classic literature of self-improvement really was improving . . . " says the Boynton character.

There is no doubt that selling, a profession that can be stressful at times, due to its emphasis on deadlines and meeting financial goals, can encourage some salespeople to engage in bad habits for relief. Some salespeople have said to me that their stressful day leads them to drinking and smoking to relax—and why is it that salespeople always seem to be hanging out in bars? Besides the outside culture's view of selling as a profession, you need to be aware of your specific organization's sales culture. One sales organization may encourage certain forms of behaviors over others, in effect reinforcing self-affirming behaviors, or, alternatively, discouraging them. Does your boss encourage cutthroat competition, browbeating salespeople to a pulp? Or constructive criticism?

It's important if you want to succeed in sales that you have a positive, upbeat, and healthy approach toward the profession and surround yourself with images and people who will support that self-affirming goal. In sales, as everywhere else, you'll know yourself by the company you keep.

Elements of a Successful Marketing Kit

Marketing Kit

- ❏ Folder with logo
- ❏ Business card
- ❏ Cover letter signed by salesperson
- ❏ Product brochure
- ❏ Product samples (if small enough)
- ❏ Direct-mail piece
- ❏ Reprints
- ❏ Publicity releases
- ❏ Copies of ads for product
- ❏ Summary of marketing efforts for product
- ❏ Fact sheets
- ❏ Product or industry research
- ❏ Newsletter
- ❏ Success stories/Return on investment sheet
- ❏ Questionnaires or checklist
- ❏ Key people backgrounder (emphasis on company expertise)
- ❏ Top ten sheet (top ten reasons to buy your product or service)

Business Letters

Letters of Introduction

Sales letters can be effective prospecting tools if you follow a few rules when writing them.

First, you need to grab the prospect's attention. Research shows that adults barely read letters. They judge whether they'll read a letter by looking at the opening and the closing first.

To attract the prospect's attention, the opening should summarize a key issue or problem that affects the client. The more personalized the opening is, the better. No one likes to feel as if she is one of a thousand people you're approaching. People like to feel special! The closer you can mirror the prospect's way of thinking, the more effective your opening will be.

The body of the text can list reasons the prospect might find it worthwhile speaking to you. Keep in mind that the objective is to get an appointment—not to sell the client through the letter. Don't oversell your product! Instead, suggest some possible motives for getting together. After outlining the prospect's challenge, present your company as the solution. Keep the language focused from the reader's perspective, enumerating the end results you can create.

The call to action at the close of the letter should be to initiate a conversation with the prospect, meet the prospect, and do more information gathering about the prospect's needs. Here you should state the next steps. Since most decisionmakers are too busy to chase after salespeople, you should assure them that you will take responsibility to follow up with a call.

Here are some more letter writing tips:

- Always address an introduction letter to the most appropriate person in the organization. Qualify that individual with a phone call first, if necessary.
- Talk directly to the person you're writing the letter to. When the person reads this letter, you want his or her head to be nodding, "Yes, that's exactly my problem."
- Keep the tone of the letter positive and upbeat; most people respond better to positives than negatives.
- Be conservative in a first letter.
- Conclude by typing your full name and title, but feel free to sign with a nickname (Ed instead of Edward).
- Include an enclosure only if you're sure it will help increase your chances of meeting with the prospect.

Introductory Letter Format

Date

Name
Title/Company
Address

Dear [name],

[Personalized attention-grabber]

Congratulations on reaching your fifth year in business. What a milestone! Although I've seen your name around town quite often, I realize that we've never really had the opportunity to sit down and talk.

[Statement of purpose]

The purpose of this letter is to introduce myself and let you know in advance that I'll be calling you next week to schedule a time to get together. As the [title] of [company] here in [location], it's my goal to personally connect with all local business owners such as yourself.

[Call to action]

I look forward to talking with you next week and setting up a time to meet.

Sincerely,

Name of sales rep
Title
[Added value]

P.S. Enclosed is a recent article I thought you might find interesting!

June 15, 2000

Mr. Jonathan White
Vice-President
First National Savings Bank
496 Main St.
Super City, U.S.A. 00001

Dear Mr. White:

Computer software programs play a key role in the efficiency of your branch managers, your internal staff, and the bank as a whole. However, struggling through manuals and learning a system can be time-consuming as well as frustrating. That's where we come in!

Software Teaching Pros (STP) is a software consulting firm dedicated to teaching your staff in the most efficient manner possible. Your branch managers, customer service representatives, and tellers learn only the programs they need, in their offices. Since 1992, STP's trained staff of fourteen software experts has been helping companies leverage their software systems to raise internal productivity and deliver higher levels of customer satisfaction.

I look forward to talking with you in regard to the types of programs your staff may currently be using, or may wish to use in the future, and how we can assist you in that process. Enclosed is a brochure with some additional information on our company. I look forward to talking with you early next week. If you have any immediate questions, please feel free to contact me directly at 1-800-111-1111.

Sincerely,

Ross Jones
Senior Account Executive

Follow-up Notes

The purpose of follow-up notes is to demonstrate that you are great at servicing your customers. Follow-up notes are an opportunity to bond with the customer by proving that you've listened to them and know who they are. Your goal is to separate yourself from the crowd, build good will, make the recipient feel important, and set the stage for a "working appointment" rather than a sales appointment.

Cold Call Follow-up Note

Date

Name
Company
Address

Dear Jennifer:

Thank you for your time today. During our brief meeting it was interesting to learn more about your company. Enclosed is the additional information you requested on our products and services.

I will give you a call early next week to schedule a time to get together to further discuss your company's situation and how I may be helpful to you.

Sincerely,

Your name
Your title

P.S. Enclosed is an article on skiing that made me think of you and that I'd thought you'd like to see. Enjoy!

Networking Follow-up Letter to an Initial Contact

Date

Name
Company
Address

Dear Terry,

It was a pleasure meeting you at the chamber of commerce event last night. I've already thanked Richard for introducing us. Based on our conversation, we are both talking to the same buyers.

I work as a resource for my customers and from time to time I may have a customer with the need for your services. I'd like to get together to learn more about your company and fill you in about the scope of my services. I'll give you a call at the end of the week to set up a coffee meeting.

I look forward to talking with you soon.

Regards,

Your name
Your title

Sample After-the-Sales-Call Letters

The purpose of this letter is to make sure the prospect understands what you expect from them and what they should expect from you. Make sure that the expectations you raise in this follow-up letter are possible to achieve. Don't promise to send something by a certain date and then not do it!

Don't forget to:

- ❑ Write the letter with the prospect's needs and perspective in mind

- ❑ Be brief and concise

- ❑ Make sure any promises you make are believable and doable

- ❑ Outline the next steps that you'll take in an organized fashion

- ❑ End with a request for action

- ❑ Give a time frame for further follow-up

- ❑ Proofread the letter for spelling, punctuation, and the accuracy of company/prospect names and titles

Date

Name
Company
Address

Dear Ruth,

Just a quick note to thank you for your time at our meeting today. It was quite interesting to learn more about [state the prospect's company name] and your specific objectives.

To clarify the next steps, you'll be faxing me the specs for this project and I will be sending you a formal proposal by the end of the week. I'll give you a call early next week to make sure you've received the proposal and to answer any questions you may have.

I look forward to working with you on this project.

Sincerely,

Your name
Your title

Sample Follow up Letter

Date

Name
Company
Address

Dear [name]:

Thanks for meeting with me today and sharing so much about [company name].

Even though you are not ready to pursue a purchase of [state your service/product] at this time, I hope that our conversation gave you some fresh ideas to try out on [state the problem] over the next few months.

I'll check back with you in two months to see how things are going. In the meantime, I wish you the best of luck with [state problem], and if I can be of assistance to you in any way, don't hesitate to call.

Thanks once again for taking time from your busy schedule to meet with me and for the information that you shared.

Sincerely,

Your name
Your title

Sample Follow up Letter

Date

Name
Company
Address

Dear [name]:

Thanks for meeting with me last week and reviewing with me in such detail what [company name] is looking to achieve in the marketplace.

As promised, I'm enclosing some information about [your service/product]. As we discussed, [your product or service] offers a well-priced alternative to the service you're currently buying [or state other benefit].

I'll call you in a few days to set up a meeting so that we can customize a proposal to suit your firm's specific needs. I feel sure that [your company name] can help you achieve [state prospect's goal]. In the meantime, please don't hesitate to call me with any questions.

Sincerely,

Your name
Your title

Sample E-mail to Existing Customer

Goals: E-mail is great for immediate follow up and to provide needed information quickly. Keep e-mail short, to the point, and avoid unnecessary chit-chat.

Hello Gary,
Just a quick note to follow up on meeting today. As always, it was great to see you. I really enjoy working together. Here's the brief punch list with time lines for you about the upcoming Time & Territory Management program for senior sales staff:

ITEM	REQUIREMENTS	DATE OF COMPLETION
Sales staff names	Gary will provide list to me	August 1
Sales staff interviews	Net-Works will make calls	August 15
Program customization	Net-Works design	August 31
Materials shipped	Gary will give contact	September 5
Program delivery	Net-Works will present program	September 15

I look forward to working together with you on this project! I'll give you a call in early August to check for any changes in your marketplace.
Nancy

Thank-You Letters

See sample thank-you letters following on pages 215 and 216.

Letter of Agreement

Note: There is no substitute for seeing an attorney and having a contract drawn up that is tailored to the needs of your business. Having said that, here's a generic letter of agreement on page 217, that at least one experienced sales rep has found useful.

Date

Name
Title/company
Address

Dear [name],

Thank you for the opportunity to work together on [state the product or service]. It's been a pleasure assisting you with [state the business objective].

Enclosed are [added value—e.g., articles, notes regarding the project, additional information, testimonials from people involved in the process], which I thought you'd enjoy seeing. I appreciate your business and will give you a call in a few weeks to check in.

I look forward to working together again soon.

Sincerely,

Name of sales rep
Title

[Handwritten is preferable]
Date

Dear [name],

Just a quick note to thank you for the referral to [state prospect's name].
As a result of your referral, I [state a result or the current status—e.g.,
scheduled an appointment, met with them]. I will keep you posted on the out-
come.
Thanks again for thinking of me and please let me know how I can be helpful
to you.

Regards,

Name of sales rep

Date

Name
Title/company
Address

Dear [name],

This letter confirms our agreement for [state product or service] to [state what is to be done] on [date]. We further agree that [your company name]'s fee will include:

A. [State terms agreed upon]
B. [State terms agreed upon]
C. [State terms agreed upon]

For this work [their company name] shall pay [your company name] in the amount of [state the fee] per [product, service, or item], a total of [state total investment required by prospect]. A deposit of [money amount] is due upon signing this agreement. The balance of [money amount] is due within [number] of days of the completion of [product or service].

Please sign both copies of this agreement. Return one copy to [your company name] with your check for [deposit money amount], and retain one copy for your records. I look forward to working together with you on this project.

Sincerely,

Name of sales rep/date_____   Prospect's name/date _____

Title _____   Prospect's company _____

APPENDIX C

Newsletter Tips

A newsletter is a great way to build a relationship with your clients. Keep in mind that the newsletter must be targeted to the clients interests or needs. If you lack professional design help, a newsletter can be as simple as a bulleted checklist of key points, news bits, and practical ideas printed on your letterhead. If you wish to produce a more sophisticated sales tool, however, here are some things to keep in mind:

❑ Clearly identify the newsletter with a large logo (up to 25 percent of the page) on the top of page 1; make sure the logo includes a reference to your company.

❑ Also on the first page, include a brief "In This Issue" box to catch the reader's attention.

❑ Open with a short welcome letter focusing on a point of key interest to your customers. Place a smiling picture of yourself nearby and add your signature at the bottom; this gives the piece a personal touch and establishes your credibility as an expert.

❑ Keep articles short, snappy, and to the point!

❑ Box off key ideas and news briefs.

❑ Make sure the editorial really interests your clients. Consider a balanced selection of topics, for example, an article about solving a critical problem, news briefs on current industry happenings, and a question-and-answer column.

❑ Don't forget to include how the customer can contact you!

Sample Telephone Call Script

There are three steps to making a telephone call:

1. *The Opening.*
    Greet and identify yourself.

2. *Body of the call.*
    Set expectations, gather information, qualify the prospect, and decide on the next steps.

3. *The close.*
    Summarize what you've learned and establish the next steps to take, such as scheduling an appointment, touching base later, and so on.

Greet and Identify
"Hello [prospective client's name], this is [full name] of [company name]. How are you today?"

Body of Call
"I noticed [explain how you've heard of them] we're both members of the chamber of commerce and [pique their interest with the promise of something new or unique] realized that we've never had an opportunity to talk. [Take the pressure off by underplaying the sales aspect of the call.] I work in [your company's market] and the reason for my call is to find out more about what you do. [People like to meet with people they have something in common with and to share information.] Do you have a few minutes?"

[If yes, proceed.]

"Tell me a little bit about your business…" [Continue with appropriate qualifying/information-gathering questions.]

"I'd like an opportunity to sit down and hear more about your business and to share with you a little bit about [what you do, your company's new business products]."

Close
"Are you free to meet next week?"

[If yes]

"That sounds great, [prospect's name]. I look forward to seeing you next Thursday at nine A.M. at your office. See you then."

[If no]

"[Prospect's name], it sounds as though you're tied up for the next few weeks. May I try you back at some future date? Thanks. When would you like me to call? Great. Then I'll call you at the beginning of June, and I look forward to meeting you then."

Sample Precall Planning Sheets

Goal: Customer data at a glance

To impress customers with your knowledge of their business concerns, you need to collect both hard data (facts and figures) and soft data (feelings and opinions). You also need to collect data that reflects both the prospect's individual perspective and the client company's overall perspective.

The generic precall planning sheet that follows is quite detailed, and you may find after trying it out on one or two customers that you can edit it down a bit. Many salespeople also develop their own ways to "code" customer information to save time. For example, some salespeople put a plus sign (+) next to prospects who have given them a favorable response in an initial conversation and a minus (-) sign when the outlook is less favorable. A dollar sign ($) can represent company size or the size of a prospective sale. Or perhaps, like other salespeople, you may find sticky colored dots useful for coding your sheet. Develop your own style, one that you can stick with and that will work for you!

PRECALL PLANNING SHEET

Company Data

Company name: _____ Date: _____

Address: _____

Telephone: _____ Fax: _____

Age of business: _____

Annual revenue: _____

Structure: _____

Geographical territory: _____

Number of employees: _____

Number of locations: _____

Products/Services: _____

Primary customers: _____

Major competitors: _____

Market environment for company's product/service: _____

Current situation: _____

Future focus: _____

Fiscal year: _____

When they plan to purchase: _____

When they make purchase: _____

Budget for purchase: _____

Currently doing business with me (Y/N)? _____

Room to increase business with me? _____

PRECALL PLANNING SHEET

Key Decisionmakers

(These may include any or all of the following: the company president/business owner; vice-president of sales; vice-president of marketing; product manager; management supervisor; purchasing director; promotion manager, advertising agency; vice-president of product development; account executive. Fill out the following information on each individual who is likely to influence whether the client will buy what you have to sell.)

Name: _____

Current position: _____

Best way to contact: _____

Best time to contact: _____

Decisionmaker's key support people (i.e., administrative assistant) and how best to contact them: _____

Role played in decision-making process: _____

Years with company: _____

Background with company: _____

Prior experience: _____

Likes/Dislikes: _____

Business community involvement: _____

Description of work style: _____

Other observations: _____

Personal information (family, interests/hobbies, personal style, born/raised, etc.) _____

Strategy considerations _____

_____

Customer's Goals: _____

_____

PRECALL PLANNING SHEET

Objections to overcome: ____________________

____

____

Critical points to cover: ____________________

____

____

What can I offer? ____________________

____

____

Added-value (things not included in the direct sale) ideas: ____________________

____

____

What the competition can offer: ____________________

____

Who I need to present to: ____________________

____

My proposal: ____________________

____

____

Specific steps I must take: ____________________

____

Proposed follow-up schedule (i.e., schedule of meetings, date proposal is due, etc.) ____________________

____

____

A Buyer's Guide to Time Management Tools, Organizational Aids, and Programs

Time is one of your most precious assets. As my aunt is fond of saying, "Waste time, and you waste your life." Fortunately, there are many tools on the market that can help you manage time effectively. To structure your sales effort and keep track of activities and clients, it's helpful to have a few business tools such as a cell phone for making calls while you're on the road, a pager/beeper so your office and clients can contact you at a moment's notice, a pocket tape recorder so you can dictate thoughts while traveling; a calendar/appointment book, an address book, and a computer (perhaps even a portable notebook or palmtop) for typing up proposals and follow-up letters, among other things.

Thousands of products and services currently on the market are designed to help you keep things organized and focus your energy. I've listed some possibilities in this appendix. I've also listed contact information for the companies that supply them. And, finally, where I could, I've listed contact information for the manufacturers, because they can always tell you what retailers in your area they supply.

Although I have used many of these items, this list is not meant to be an endorsement. You will still have to consider your particular needs, research the items, and evaluate whether they may be right for you. Nor is it a complete list, so don't hesitate to check out *Consumer Reports* or some of the technology and business magazines' buyer's guides to see if something better suits your needs. Also keep in mind that technology, software, and manufacturing is changing rapidly as time effectively speeds up in our "the future is now" society. Although this information was current as of press time, you may not find everything on the list at the moment you happen to read the book. Then again, you may find something better—new technology is coming on the market all the time!

Training for the Technologically Challenged

Sales is a profession that frequently attracts people who want to work with other people. Many salespeople are outgoing individuals who like to have personal contact with clients. I've noticed that people who think of themselves as "people" people often shy away from using software programs, computers, and so on. If you're one of them, you'll notice that many items on the following list are programs, computers, or computer-like things that may give rise to a degree of technophobia. Before you dismiss these technical aids, give some thought to why you are dismissing them. Technology is the wave of the future, and sooner or later, most of us who need to communicate with others on a regular basis will have to deal with it. Do you find that thought daunting? Perhaps you're asking yourself when you will find the time to learn about things like the Internet, and who can help you? Buying a program does not guarantee that you can use it. Who can teach you how to use a program for a reasonable fee?

Here are two suggestions. First, *visit your local library.* Libraries today are information centers equipped with computers that have access to the Internet. If you are not hooked up, you can get a feel for what it's like by trying it out at the library. Ask a reference librarian to help you look up some of the Web sites listed in this appendix.

Second, *sign up for on-line learning.* As a salesperson, you want to keep track of leads, correspondence, and client information in the most efficient way possible. You'd like to use ACT, one of the best-selling contract managers, to handle your sales accounts, but you're afraid you won't be able to learn to use it on your own and will give up in frustration before it does you any good. Wouldn't it be nice to have a training coach at your disposal, any time, day or night, who could show you exactly what to do visually on the screen as if the program were up and running?

That's the idea behind LearnItOnline, an on-line classroom developed by publisher Ziff-Davis. Offering an integrated system of print, on-line, and broadcast media, Ziff-Davis has aggressively entered the computing education field with the launch of LearnItOnline. It is a community-based (many community colleges offer it) distance learning resource that is geared to enable the everyday business professional to train in the use of a number of the popular computer programs—right in the comfort of his or her office or home—any time, day or night. Once you pay a modest fee and you're registered, you'll be able to dial up the Ziff-Davis Zdnet University (ZDU), the on-line campus for continuing education in technology, and access interactive tutorials for a variety of popular administrative programs.

The tutorials are easy to navigate as long as you know how to point a mouse and click. The courses are designed to deliver the actual look and feel of working within an application. A skills assessment program helps users customize the curriculum and personalize their training plan. Each course consists of approximately ten to thirty training tutorials that cover specific topics in ten to twenty minutes. This structure allows students to formulate a convenient study schedule according to their specific needs. Students can cover as much or as little as they choose at any given time, any day, from any remote location. And, because the tutorials are designed as if you were using the actual program (unlike some software training CDs), the LearnItOnline modules don't require you to have a particular program installed on your computer to train in how to use it. So, another plus is that if you want to get a feel for using a particular program before you buy it, you can. The tutorials are designed for the general business person who has little or no computer skill. The courses automatically guide users through the software, highlighting critical components and important short cuts, while showing how to make the most efficient use of the product.

Current tutorial offerings include ACT (a popular account tracking and sales management program), 1-2-3 Millennium Edition, HTML Programming, Microsoft Exchange Client, Notes, GroupWise, Microsoft Office (Access, Excel, PowerPoint, Word for Windows, Outlook); Windows 95, Windows 98, Windows NT, Quicken Deluxe, Microsoft Project 98, Front Page, Internet Explorer, Netscape Navigator, Netscape Communicator, and WordPerfect. Students can enroll in as many courses as they wish for an annual subscription fee. As of press time, the subscription cost $75 through my local community college. (I'll talk a little bit more about which computer programs may be most helpful for salespeople in the section on Sales Training.

Ziff-Davis
28 East 28th Street
New York, New York 10016-7930
212-503-3500
www.learnitonline.com
www.zdnet.com

Office Supply Retailers and Catalogs

The following companies sell office supplies and equipment, including a variety of organizers, planners, software, office furniture, and computers. Most have retail stores and catalogs. QVC offers television sales as well as sales information via a Web site. Some of these retailers have useful information on their Web site. For example, Office Depot allows you to download free business forms and provides tips for people in business.

Daymark: 1-800-729-9000
Office Depot: 800-685-8800; www.officedepot.com
OfficeMax: 800-788-8080; 800-283-7674; www.officemax.com
QVC: 888-345-5788; www.qvc.com
Staples: 800-333-3330; www.staples.com

Plannners

Today, as more people lead busier and, we hope, more fulfilling lives, companies producing appointment books and day organizers have proliferated. It's hard to realize that day planners didn't always crowd the store shelves. Back in the 1940s, attorney Morris Perkin decided that the appointment calendar he was using wasn't giving him enough information about his working day. Perkin designed his own work planner and organizer featuring a calendar, appointment book, time record, and a tickler reminder system. Called Lawyer's Day, Perkin was soon marketing his personal solution to time management to other professionals. Perkin worked with a Pennsylvania printer to produce and market this system that would become the prototype for a number of planners designed to be used by other professionals. In time the planning system became generic for all professions and was dubbed the "Day-Timer system."

According to the Day-Timer Web site, Perkin showed potential customers that lawyers who used the system earned 50 percent more than those who didn't. That's a telling statistic for today's professionals, who have even less time than their predecessors.

Some of the companies I've listed only manufacture organizers; others have branched out and offer time management and other

educational seminars, in addition to self-help books and tapes. Another new trend is that many of these companies offer digital or computer versions of their workday planners. Check the retailers listed here. Most carry these planners. If not, contact the manufacturers directly, since most offer catalogues as well as take orders through their Web sites. Time management tips, seminar schedules, and links to other relevant sites are some of the "extras" you'll find on their Web sites.

Day-Timers

Day-Timers, Inc. of Allentown, Pennsylvania, manufactures the modern-day version of the Perkin planner. Day-Timer Technologies, an expansion of Day-Timers, Inc., produces a personal organizer software program, Day-Timer Organizer, which uses the Day-Timer paper planner formats, and prints to Day-Timer pages. Day-Timers also makes home organization software, Day-Timer HomeLife, designed to help busy households manage their time better. In 1997 the company entered into a product development venture with Sharp Electronics, and introduced Day-Timer Organizer software bundled with a palmtop, the Sharp Wizard.

Day-Timers, Inc.
One Day-Timer Plaza
Allentown, PA 19155-1551
800-225-5005
888-972-0800
www.daytimers.com

Franklin Covey

Franklin Covey publishes an organizer called the Franklin Planner, which uses positive affirmations, inspirational sayings, and life principles to reinforce the ideas summarized in Stephen Covey's book, *The Seven Habits of Highly Effective People*. The company also offers a computer software program designed to help clients retain and use Franklin Covey concepts and skills. The company's products are available in thirty-two languages. A line of products developed by the company and other products selected and endorsed by Franklin Covey are available in more than 130 Franklin Covey stores throughout North America and in several other countries.

Franklin Covey
2200 West Parkway Blvd.
Salt Lake City, Utah 84119
800-654-1776
www.franklincovey.com

Other Sources.

Here are several other sources for planners and other organizational tools.

At-A-Glance
101 O'Neil Road
Sidney, NY 13838-1099
607-563-1761
607-563-8811
888-302-4155
www.ataglance.com

Day Runner, Inc.
15295 Alton Parkway
Irvine, CA 92718
800-232-9798
www.dayrunner.com

Filofax, Inc.
372 Danbury Rd.
Suite 171
Wilton, Ct.
203-563-2200
www.filofax.com

For business card/address files:
Rolodex
800-446-5652
www.rolodex.com

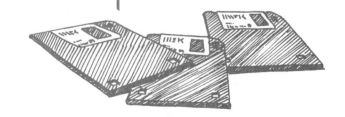

Sales Training, Support Groups, and Other Self-Empowerment Seminars

Here is a list of training programs that you may find useful. I have taken some of these programs; others have been recommended by friends or through other means. There are many sales training and self-improvement programs on the market, so feel free to explore them. Just because a program isn't on this list doesn't mean you might not find it helpful.

As with any monetary investment, make sure the goal of the program you choose respects your personal objectives and emphasizes setting your own goals, rather than following arbitrary rules dictated by the training organization. I've found it helpful to experiment with a variety of training systems, not only because each system has something a little different to offer, but because it keeps the process fresh.

Two days after attending most seminars, even very good ones, most participants can barely remember a few maxims. For permanent change to take place, anyone who aims for self-improvement through self-empowerment needs constant reinforcement and practice putting what has been learned to use in the real world. Ask about maintenance plans, follow-up coaching, and/or ongoing coaching opportunities, as well as books or tapes that can assist you in maintaining the training experience in the weeks and months after taking a seminar or workshop.

Anthony Robbins

Anthony Robbins's Anthony Robbins Companies offer seminars, books, videotapes, cassettes, and CD-ROMs outlining philosophies and techniques for personal and professional development. Personal Power, Unleash the Power Within, Power Talk, The Competitive Edge, Life Mastery, Date with Destiny, Wealth Mastery, Leadership Mastery, The Body You Deserve, Unlimited Power, and Lessons in Mastery are all programs that have inspired thousands of people to explore the possibility of a more successful future. Robbins's O.P.A. Life Management System™ emphasizes getting more from life by making a fundamental shift from time management to life management.

In creating these programs, Robbins has interviewed what he calls "masters" of influence, business, and personal finance, so he could share their ideas, principles, and actions for success with his own clients and customers. His programs are designed to give people a workable system to be used daily in order to achieve the same extraordinary success he has. Robbins focuses on ways people can motivate themselves to achieve a peak mindset through neuroassociative conditioning and maintaining passion for personal goals.

The Robbins Results Coaching partnership provides support in attaining results in life, much the same way a personal fitness trainer assists a person in achieving physical empowerment.

Anthony Robbins Companies: 800-898-8669
www.anthonyrobbins.com

Dale Carnegie

Dale Carnegie is still an American legend nearly half a century after his death in 1955. A salesman for Armour and Company who set out to teach people how to overcome their fear of public speaking, he became famous for showing others how to become successful. Carnegie's book *How to Win Friends and Influence People* (1936) has sold more than 10 million copies and has been translated the world over. His philosophy is: Believe that you will succeed, and you will.

Dale Carnegie Training® carries on his philosophy by helping people in corporations sharpen their skills and improve their performance. The training focuses on practical principles and processes to develop employees' innate abilities. Programs are targeted toward corporate organizations seeking employee development in strategic areas and toward individuals who want to strengthen their professional performance.

The curriculum is based on what the company describes as a proprietary four-phase continuous improvement that addresses:

- Developing leadership
- Increasing productivity
- Building strong teams
- Improving communications
- Unleashing creativity
- Excelling at customer service

A priority of the Dale Carnegie training programs is to focus on everyday, real-world problems, and to emphasize behavior-based solutions, practical applications, and measurable results. Training requires participants to apply what they're learning to real-world business situations as well as to the client company's current business strategy and long-range corporate vision.

Programs include Individual Solutions, an open-enrollment program for individuals. Courses include The Dale Carnegie Course, Sales Advantage, and Leadership Training for Managers. Programs are offered in twenty languages. They cover defining goals, setting priorities, communicating better, increasing your productivity, excelling in challenging situations, and developing your leadership skills.

Dale Carnegie
www.dalecarnegie.com

Day-Timers, Inc.

In the late 1970s, a Mormon minister, Charles Hobbs, who advocated that time management was the key to a healthy and balanced life, discovered the Day-Timer planner and began using it in his time management seminars. In the 1980s, Day-Timers bought out Hobbs and acquired the rights to Time Power, a series of books and tapes related to time management, and entered the field of time management seminars. Today the company offers 4-Dimensional Time Management, a training seminar geared toward helping people achieve balance. The seminar shows people how to clarify their varying roles and responsibilities and then to achieve balance by prioritizing them. Next, they help clients set personal and cooperative goals, and show them how teaming up with people in both personal and professional areas of life creates a synergy that allows them to achieve more. The goal is to enable participants to free up as much as six hours per work week to use for their top personal priorities and at the same time to increase productivity by up to 30 percent.

Day-Timers, Inc.: 888-972-0800, 800-225-5005
www.daytimers.com

Dialogue House/The Intensive Journal Workshop

Learning to create passion in our lives, to build a spiritual base, to know ourselves well so that we can identify personal principles and goals, and to be able to calm ourselves during stressful times are ongoing themes in many sales workshops and personal empowerment–training sessions. The Intensive Journal Workshop offers a unique journal-based approach to tackling these issues.

Starting in the 1950s, Dr. Ira Progoff, a leading authority on C. G. Jung, several forms of psychology, and journal writing, began to explore the uses of journal writing to enhance personal growth. (The depth psychological approach believes that all forms of consciousness are related and that the psyche is present in nature.) Director of the Institute for Research in Depth Psychology at Drew University from 1959 to 1971, Dr. Progoff conducted research on how individuals develop more fulfilling lives. He discovered that people who kept a journal worked through issues more rapidly than those who didn't. Dr. Progoff then developed and refined the Intensive Journal Method to provide a way to mirror the processes by which people become self-empowered to develop themselves. He conducted workshops in the process, refining the method before publishing the process in a book titled *At a Journal Workshop*.

Later Progoff added a related component—process meditation—and formed the Intensive Journal Program to make workshops available to the public through trained and certified leaders. Dr. Progoff passed away in 1998, but workshops in his methods continue to be produced by Dialogue House.

The goal of the Intensive Journal Program is to help those who use it to gain insights into different areas of their lives, including their career, personal relationships, and health. Participants work step-by-step through exercises in the Intensive Journal workbook. Through Journal Feedback, a continuous process of writing and reading back entries (to themselves—participants are the only ones who read their own journals), participants create a dynamic process that helps them recognize the challenges they face, develop insight

about their career and other issues, and build the internal momentum to make positive life changes and manage stress.

Through journaling and meditation, participants are encouraged to explore symbols and metaphors that are meaningful to them. These images, combined with the journal process, enable participants to access inner resources, enhancing communication and management skills, developing the ability to relate and adapt to new people and environments, develop and use intuition, identify skills and interests to become more productive, and calm the mind.

In addition to workshops, cassettes featuring meditations recorded by Dr. Progoff and his book, *At A Journal Workshop*, are available.

Dialogue House
80 E. 11th Street, Suite 305
New York, NY, 10003
800-221-5844
212-673-5880
e-mail: info@intensivejournal.org

Franklin Covey

Franklin Covey's training is based on the principles outlined in Stephen R. Covey's book, *The Seven Habits of Highly Effective People*. These principles focus on character ethic (i.e., basic principles of effective living), as the foundation of success. The company teaches people to look inside out, and to teach themselves independently of any company. The Franklin Covey approach addresses habits of effectiveness at four levels: personal, interpersonal, managerial, and organizational. The philosophy is that efforts applied to one area support efforts in another. Another principle is that effective people create effective organizations. Because individuals create strategies aligned to the mission and vision of the organization and the needs of the marketplace, organizational change and improvement must first come from people.

Franklin Covey empowerment programs are conducted at company facilities in the Rocky Mountains of Utah as well as on-site at client locations and through open enrollment workshops and speeches in more than four hundred cities in North America and forty countries worldwide. Consulting services, personal coaching, custom on-site training, and client-facilitated training are among the offerings. In addition to the Franklin Planner, the company offers a wide variety of audiotapes and videotapes, books, and computer software programs to help clients maintain skills.

Programs include Time and Life Management, Leadership Development; Effective Communications, Principle-Centered Organizational Change, Project and Workload Management, Performance Consulting, Time and Project Management, What Matters Most, What Matters Most for Palm Computing Organizers, Planning for Results, Leadership and Change Management Overview, The 7 Habits of Highly Effective People Workshops, Principle-Centered Leadership Week!, Measuring the Impact of Learning and Performance, Communication Solutions Building Trust!, Power of Understanding!, Getting to Synergy!, Writing Advantage, Presentation Advantage!, Meeting Advantage!, Organizational Effectiveness Cycle, Organizational Health Assessment, and Rethinking Stress.

> Covey Personal Coaching Division
> 2200 W. Parkway Blvd.
> Salt Lake City, UT 84119
> 800-333-5136, Ext. 10
> To speak directly with a Franklin Covey associate,
>   call (800) 882-6839.

The Optimist Club

Unlike the other entries on this list, the Optimist Club International (OCI) is not a training program, but rather a club devoted to principles that are useful for any salesperson to maintain. Founded in 1911 and currently one of the largest and most active service club organizations in the world, OCI is comprised of more than 155,000 volunteer members in 4,200 Optimist Clubs.

The primary goal of the club is to develop optimism as a philosophy of life—something every salesperson surely needs help with! Beyond that, OCI members are encouraged to focus on many worthwhile goals: to promote an active interest in good government and civic affairs, to work for international accord and friendship among

all people, and to aid and encourage the development of youth. OCI members believe that the giving of one's self in service to others will advance the well-being of humanity, the community, and the world. Fostering an optimistic way of life leads to the improvement of individuals and society. Personal development is a club priority. OCI offers its members many opportunities to gain leadership experience and to grow personally and professionally as they build social and business relationships with individuals from a cross section of their communities.

The power of positive thinking informs all Optimist programs. Optimist Clubs conduct service programs tailored to local community needs. They create their own service programs as well as select programs from a menu of international programs of service. The Optimists develop corporate partnerships with community-minded businesses to help fund their service efforts—offering savvy businesspeople the opportunity to network with like-minded individuals. Optimists believe that through positive action in their communities they can create a better tomorrow—sounds like a great mission statement for a salesperson, too!

Membership to OCI includes a subscription to *The Optimist*, the official publication of Optimist International, published six times annually. If you want to be a part of a group that collectively fosters a positive mental attitude, it should be relatively easy.

Optimist International
4494 Lindell Boulevard
St. Louis, Missouri 63108
800-678-8389
314-371-6000
www.optimist.org
E-mail OCI at headquarters@optimist.org
1-800-OPT-8389, ext. 0
314-371-6000

Sandler Sales Institute

David Sandler began developing his sales training system in the late 1960s and early 1970s, focusing on small and mid-sized companies, Fortune 500 corporations, and individual nonselling professionals. In 1983 he began franchising his proprietary training pro-grams as the Sandler Sales Institute. In 1995, David Sandler died, but his legacy lives on a national network of trainers. Today, the Sandler Sales Institute offers training to companies and individuals in the fields of sales, management, consulting, and leadership development through ongoing seminars and workshops put on by a network of certified trainers and professional consultants.

The Sandler approach is based on the belief that traditional selling techniques simply don't work anymore and the result is that prospects control a sale and destroy a salesperson's self-esteem in the process. The Sandler Sales Institute's motto is Break the rules and close more sales! The goal is to empower the sales-person to control the selling process with no-nonsense, results-driven sales techniques. Two publications reveal more about the Sandler method: *You Can't Teach a Kid to Ride a Bike at a Seminar* by David Sandler and *Close the Deal* by Sandler with Sam Deep and Lyle Sussman.

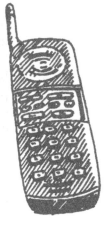

Sandler offers short-term training to pinpoint specific business issues and ongoing training for lasting change and to reinforce success.

The Institute's President's Club provides ongoing sales training and reinforcement comprised of skill building, mutual support, and personal coaching, and offers members networking opportunities with other business owners, salespeople, and managers. Sales Strategies for Non-Selling Professionals offers hands-on training designed for accountants, engineers, lawyers, and anyone who needs to build a client base for their services. Pro Summit is a modular sales training program that can be customized for firms at various stages of development. Sandler's corporate training program provides on-site training. Sales Management Training, Quality Service and Presenting Yourself round out the offerings.

Sales materials include workbooks, tapes, and a newsletter that clients can use to refresh and reinforce their training. The Web site address is www.sandler.com.

Self-Talk: A Technology for Success

The Self-Talk Solution is the work of Dr. Shad Helmstetter, author of *What to Say When You Talk to Your Self*, which has sold

over a million copies worldwide. A bestselling author, syndicated columnist, national cable television program lecturer, and behavioral researcher for twenty-five years in the field of motivational psychology, Dr. Helmstetter developed the concept of Self-Talk after analyzing why many self-improvement approaches don't succeed.

The Self-Talk approach is based on the idea that, while the majority of what happens to us in life depends on our behavior, many of us don't do the things that will result in reaching our ideals and goals for leading a happy, successful life. The reason? Our behavior depends on our beliefs; if you believe, consciously or unconsciously, that you are "never going to succeed at sales," then you won't. These beliefs come from programming that we receive from the world around us. The brain converts sensory information into new beliefs, but it does so based on experiences, which often are not objective. Thus, many of our beliefs are false. For example, one person might not feel safe around dogs, because he was bitten by a dog; yet, statistically, most people are not bitten by dogs. In the same way, many of us hold incorrect beliefs about ourselves that limit us from reaching our true potential—words we heard from parents, teachers, friends, and strangers that became self-fulfilling prophecies.

Self-Talk allows people to take back control of their lives by teaching them what to say when they talk to themselves. The Self-Talk program shows people how to recondition themselves using positive examples of self-talk. Self-Talk has been used to train commercial airline pilots, sports figures, and managers and salespeople. Unlike hypnosis or subliminal programming, Self-Talk depends on the trainee's consciously hearing every word, repeatedly, until it becomes familiar. Dr. Helmstetter has developed Self-Talk cassettes as a method of conditioning the brain to the language of success through repetition. The ultimate goal is for the new, positive beliefs to become internalized.

Topics covered by the Self-Talk cassettes include Self, Taking Control of Your Life, Health and Fitness, Career Achievement, Financial Success, Positive Relationships, and Personal Development. The Web site address is www.Self-Talk.com.

Zig Ziglar

The author of fifteen books on sales, personal growth, and successful living, Zig Ziglar is a well-known personal empowerment lecturer and is considered to be an authority on balancing one's life in order to achieve one's aspirations. His philosophy is one of hard work, commitment, practicality, and ethics. Ziglar believes that persistent effort combined with good character is the way to obtain things money can buy, and, more important, the things it can't. Ziglar Training Systems offers public seminars, customized educational programs, videotapes, workshops and keynote speakers focused on personal and professional development. His books and tapes have been translated into over thirty-two languages and dialects and are widely available.

Ziglar's Sales training package covers building customer trust, examining customer needs, selling benefits, closing the sale, overcoming objections, up-selling, value-added selling, team development, creating a supportive and positive atmosphere, working with difficult people, handling confrontation, dealing with pressure and deadlines, and much more. Other topics covered by Ziglar training sessions are beating stress, getting past resistance to change, staying positive in a negative world, developing successful relationships, and balancing between home and work.

Ziglar Training Systems
2009 Chenault, Suite 100
Carrollton, TX 75006
800-527-0306
972-233-9191
info@zigziglar.com

Computer Hardware

Palmtops

Palmtops are small, handheld computers that fit easily into a pocket, purse, or briefcase. Also called personal digital assistants (PDAs), they come outfitted with a variety of organizing options, among them calculators, address books, calendars, diaries, notebooks, and more. They also come with varying amounts of memory.

Prices start at less than $25 and increase to $500 or more for highly sophisticated models. Palmtops with more memory and features tend to cost more. Some models can have additional software or memory loaded through cards. For example, accessories may include attachments that allow the information in the handheld computer to be downloaded to a larger personal computer (PC), to send faxes, and more. They're convenient—and addictive, some people say—once you've got one. They eliminate paperwork, can be carried in a pocket or purse, and, together with a cell phone, represent a mini-office on the road, enabling you to send and receive faxes from your car! And many come with databases and account tracking software, so you always have your sales leads with you. The following list describes some of the currently popular palmtops. Shop for them at one of the places listed under Office Supply Retailers on page 235. Before purchasing any palmtop, ask about the features mentioned in the features checklist.

PALMTOP FEATURES CHECKLIST

When shopping for a palmtop, you'll want to compare the price to the number of features the unit has. Features that you should ask about include:

- ❑ Size
- ❑ Protective cover
- ❑ Ease of typing on keyboard
- ❑ Weight

Screen

- ❑ Clarity
- ❑ Size of screen
- ❑ Color or black-and-white
- ❑ Touchscreen
- ❑ Resolution
- ❑ Pen-based or typing
- ❑ Stylus and screen pad

Built-in Software

- ❑ Scheduling/appointments
- ❑ Telephone and address book
- ❑ To-Do list
- ❑ Anniversary and/ or important date reminder

- ❑ Home/world clocks
- ❑ Alarm

- ❑ Calendar
- ❑ Calculator with metric/currency converter
- ❑ E-mail and Internet accessible
- ❑ Fax
- ❑ Printer
- ❑ Downloadable to Windows and/or MAC
- ❑ Length of time before battery replacement

- ❑ Rechargeable battery pack
- ❑ Data protection and backup
- ❑ Infrared data transfer to other computerized devices (for example, your primary PC)
- ❑ Audio speaker to play back your sound files and voice memos
- ❑ Memory
- ❑ Digital voice recorder
- ❑ Handwriting recognition
- ❑ Upgradeable memory

Software Programs for Optional Installation (via a card or other means)

- ❑ Financial
- ❑ Checking account transactions
- ❑ Sortable
- ❑ Searching
- ❑ Password protection
- ❑ Account management

Manufacturers and Models

Below is a list of computerized organizers. Please note that the world of handheld digital personal assistants is volatile—new models and schedules are coming out all the time. So, don't be surprised if the below list isn't quite up-to-date. However, at least it will give you some idea of the possibilities out there.

Franklin Rolodex

Franklin Electronic Publishers, Inc. makes handheld electronic books and the Rolodex Electronics brand of personal information management products. Their electronic planners retail starting under $25, and features include organizing contacts, phone numbers and schedules, a calculator with metric/currency converter, home/world clocks, password, and a perpetual calendar.

Hewlett Packard

The company makes a Business Consultant that retails for under $200. It performs financial computations, including checking account transactions; advanced math and statistics functions, including cash-flow analysis; time and data management; and an easy-to-read sortable address book. A built-in interface to HP infrared printer.

Oregon Scientific

To manage business, Internet, and travel information—and with data compression for added capacity—this databank features a three-line backlit display and a unique bookmark directory that stores Internet and e-mail addresses. It provides easy one-touch access to organizer functions, including phone directory, schedule, calculator, currency/metric conversions, password and memo modes, scheduled alarms, time, and more. It has an optional PC link for data transfer. The company's Data Link Organizer costs less than $25.

Royal

Royal makes Personal Organizers for under $25 that offer features such as dual enhanced telephone numbers; built-in ten-digit calculator; trilingual operation with English, French, and Spanish modes; schedule calendar; memo memory; e-mail symbols; built-in clock and metric conversion, password security.

Seiko

For under $25, the Seiko Personal Organizer features an FM radio, appointment and telephone books, a calculator, clock, calendar, memo file, and password protection.

Sharp

Sharp Electronics offers a variety of personal organizers for between $99 and $500. The Sharp SE-500 Personal Mobile Organizer records expenses, contacts, activities, memos, and files. It features a calculator, clock, built-in modem with Internet e-mail software, an infrared port that gives it downloadability from PC Windows, and a screen that you can handwrite notes on with a stylus. Other features include three telephone files, three user files, and a reminder alarm. In addition, a three-month, weekly, or daily calendar display, a schedule keeper, and to-do list are offered. The unit allows word processing, has fax/modem and software, and wireless infrared communications. There's an optional interface for printers, faxes, and PCs/MACs. Sharp's TelMail is a fast, easy way to send and receive e-mail and to send faxes. It has 512K memory, stores five hundred messages, has a calendar and a phone book, and offers powerful search features to locate information quickly. An optional PC Link Kit offers Day-Timer Organizer and IntelliSync software plus a docking station for PC connectivity.

Texas Instruments

The Texas Instruments 8KB Data Bank/Scheduler retails for $34.80. It offers 8KB memory (enough to store over five hundred entries) and a telephone file, scheduler, clock, ten English/metric conversions, a calendar mode that displays day of the week and year for any schedule entry, and a secret password for security. The unit features an automatic power down.

Uniden

The Uniden Digital Assistant retails for $279.25. It records schedules, notes, addresses, phone numbers, e-mail, a 28.8K internal modem, voice recorder, note taker, compact flash slot for extra memory, active sync personal docking station to automatically update your files to your computer, and a Windows CE operating system.

Phillips

The Nino 510 palm-size PC keeps you up-to-date when you're on the go for about $500. The lightweight, pen-based, palm-size PC offers the added clarity of a color screen. The Nino 510 keeps track of schedules, contacts, tasks, e-mail, and Internet Information Services. The Transmissive Color Touch Screen Display supports 256 colors. With the Automatic Synchronization and Rechargeable Battery Pack, the Nino 500 can run up to eight hours on a NiMH rechargeable battery pack, or on two AA-size batteries. A rechargeable, nonremovable lithium backup battery keeps data safe. The Infrared (IrDA)Transceiver allows you to transfer information up to 115Kbps. You can send files or messages to other Microsoft Windows CE devices or synchronize with your primary PC. An audio speaker lets you play back your sound files and voice memos with optimum sound. It has a memory of 16MB RAM, a digital voice recorder, and handwriting recognition.

3Com

The Palm Pilot III organizer is the third generation of small, smart organizers from 3Com. Its most sophisticated version stores 12,000 addresses, 5 years of appointments, 3,000 "to-do" items, and 400 e-mails. It has 4MB RAM; a new, clearer display screen that's less reflective in bright sunlight; and includes a MS outlook conduit. It is memory upgrade capable—up to 8 MB. The 3Com Palm V Connected Organizer retails for $200 to $500.

Compaq

The Compaq Aero 2130 Palm Sized PC features a 256-color screen; rechargeable lithium ion batteries (up to ten hours of life); a 16MB memory (upgradeable to 24MB); an integrated speaker; a headphone jack and external microphone jack; one-touch instant record button; and seamless synchronization with your PC. The Compaq Aero 2130 Palm Sized PC retails for $499.99.

Royal

The Royal Davinci Personal Digital Assistant retails for $99.99. It stores thousands of items and features handwriting recognition, optional plug-in folding keyboard, synchronize data with your PC, telephone, to-do, planner and calendar.

Proposal Questionnaire

Proposals are based on three things:

1. objectives
2. strategies
3. actions

The following letter and sample questionnaire are designed to help you structure an effective client proposal.

Sample Proposal Letter

Date

Name
Title/Company
Address

Dear [name],

It was a pleasure meeting with you yesterday and learning more about [prospect's name]. Based on our conversation, you are looking for [state product or service] to meet the following three objectives:

Increase [state prospect's desired result]
Enhance [state prospect's desired result]
Develop [state prospect's desired result]

As we discussed, to best accomplish your goals, our [product or service] will best suit your needs. Enclosed are the specifications tailored to your situation. The financial investment for [this specific product or service being proposed] is [state total dollar amount]. This investment includes [list related value-added items—e.g., research, materials, labor]. I look forward to talking with you further about this project.

Sincerely,

Name of Sales Rep
Title

cc: [Copy appropriate people]

1. Decisionmakers to present to:

2. List the client's goals:

3. List the clients needs:

4. How does the current industry/market environment impact these objectives?

5. What opportunities is the client able to take advantage of at this time, that he or she may not later?

6. Why is the timing right to buy?

7. Why is it important for the client to act now?

8. Summarize your key idea for this client:

9. Why will your idea work? How does it address:

   ❑ Client goals

   ❑ Client needs

   ❑ Market environment

   ❑ Timing considerations

   ❑ Client's position compared to competitors

10. What extra benefits will your idea bring to the client?

11. How is what you have to offer unique?

12. What proof can you offer that your proposed idea will help the client to achieve your goal? (Surveys, satisfied client testimonials, case studies, etc.)

13. Briefly summarize your proposal in concrete terms (What are they buying? How much will it cost?): "If you [state key idea], you will [state benefit], as proved by [state proof]."

14. Ask the client to take action. Describe the next step, for example, ask for the sale.

Forms

Territory Analysis

To get a handle on the worth of your territory (i.e., potential revenue and income), add up the dollar value of your potential business. If your territory is large or if you're just getting started, including all possible sources of revenue can be overwhelming. The task will seem more manageable if you focus on assembling a list of priority accounts, say the top twenty possibilities in each of three areas: Existing Business, Competitor's Business, and New Business (belonging neither to you nor to your competitor). Throughout the selling cycle, you should constantly be monitoring your goal lists, adding new priorities as some potentials say no and converting New Business yeses to Existing Business, so that over the course of the selling period the existing client business list grows.

Salesperson: _____   Date: _____

Existing Business

Top 20 Revenue Sources	1998($)	1999($)	Goal($)
1.			
2.			
3.			
4.			
5.			
6.			
7.			
8.			
9.			
10			
11.			
12.			
13.			
14.			
15.			
16.			
17.			
18.			
19.			
20.			

TERRITORY ANALYSIS

Competitor's Business

Top 20 Accounts	Current Value ($)
1.	
2.	
3.	
4.	
5.	
6.	
7.	
8.	
9.	
10.	
11.	
12.	
13.	
14.	
15.	
16.	
17.	
18.	
19.	
20.	

New Business

Top 20 Sources	Current Value ($)
1.	
2.	
3.	
4.	
5.	
6.	
7.	
8.	
9.	
10.	
11.	
12.	
13.	
14.	
15.	
16.	
17.	
18.	
19.	
20.	

Basic Market Summary:

$ _____ Existing Business $ _____ New Business (Not Included in Competitor's List)

$ _____ Competitor's Business $ _____ TOTAL REVENUE (Potential of List at Start of Sales Cycle

CALL REPORT SHEET

Call Report Form

Person _____ Issue _____ Page_____ of _____

ACCOUNT	CATEGORY	PROJECTED SALE	$	%	PROGRESS (Date/Contact/Purpose/Result)	FINAL SALE

Received From: _____ Date _____ Total $ _____

Pages _____

Remarks: _____

Sales Activity Report

Client Name: _____ AE _____

DATE	ACTION TAKEN	RESULTS/COMMENTS	FOLLOW-UP

CREDIT REPORT FORM

YOUR LOGO	**YOUR ADDRESS, PHONE, & FAX #:** _____ _____
	SALESPERSON: _____

CLIENT CREDIT REFERENCE FORM

COMPANY NAME: _____

BUSINESS LOCATION ADDRESS: _____

MAILING ADDRESS: _____

BUSINESS PHONE: _____ **FAX:** _____ **AX#:** _____

❑ Business is a Corporation
  Corporation name if different than above: _____
  State & Date of Incorporation: _____
❑ Business is a Proprietorship
  How long at present address: _____

Name of Principal: _____
Residence Address: _____
Residence Phone: _____
Principal's Social Security #: _____
Other Principal Parties: _____

BANK REFERENCES

Name/Branch	Complete Address	Phone#
1.		
2.		

TRADE REFERENCES

Name	Complete Address	Phone#
1.		
2.		
3.		

I/We hereby give *Your Company Name* permission to inquire of the above references or any other references that may be necessary for the Credit Department to establish credit for the above-named business. By accepting credit, if offered, I agree to the terms and conditions incorporated in the *Your Company Name* purchase contract. In consideration of the extension of credit to the Applicant, the undersigned individual Personal Guarantor jointly and severally guarantee the payment of any amount due under the terms and conditions set forth in the *Your Company Name* purchase contract.

Signature Applicant: _____

Title: _____ Name: _____

Date _____

YES, YES, YES...I WANT TO INCREASE MY BUSINESS

❑ Yes! Please add me to your mailing list at the address below. Send me your free quarterly newsletter immediately so I may learn more about how your products and services can help my business grow.

❑ Yes! Please call me at the number below. My company is interested in your products or services and would like to talk directly to you.

❑ Yes! Please call me at the number below. I know of another organization that would be interested in a speaker on this subject.

Name: _____

Title: _____

Company: _____

Address: _____

_____

_____

Telephone: _____

Fax: _____

Index

EVERYTHING

The Everything Money Book
by Rich Mintzer with Kathi Mintzer, C.P.A.

The Everything Money Book is written simply to make handling, managing, saving, and possibly earning money easier. It provides suggestions so that anyone can achieve their financial goals: whether it s sending the kids to college, planning a superb vacation, or retiring in another state. The information is shared in easy-to-follow language, so even the first-time budgeter won t be overwhelmed.

Trade paperback, $12.95
1-58062-145-7, 288 pages

The Everything Online Business Book
by Rob Liflander

If you are a small business or home business owner and are looking to establish a presence on the Web, you need *The Everything Online Business Book*. Covering every aspect of the technical process, the book outlines instructions on site development and design, programming, and accessing the hottest interactive features. In addition, each component of creating an online business, including sales and marketing, customer service, and financing is fully detailed. Move your existing business into the future with *The Everything Online Business Book*!

Trade paperback, $12.95
1-58062-320-4, 304 pages

Available Wherever Books Are Sold

If you cannot find these titles at your favorite retail outlet, you may order them directly from the publisher. BY PHONE: Call 1-800-872-5627. We accept Visa, MasterCard, and American Express. $4.95 will be added to your total order for shipping and handling. BY MAIL: Write out the full titles of the books you d like to order and send payment, including $4.95 for shipping and handling, to: Adams Media Corporation, 260 Center Street, Holbrook, MA 02343. 30-day money-back guarantee.

We Have EVERYTHING

I ♥ EVERYTHING

More Bestselling Everything Titles Available From Your Local Bookseller:

Everything **After College Book**
Everything **Astrology Book**
Everything **Baby Names Book**
Everything **Baby Shower Book**
Everything **Barbeque Cookbook**
Everything® **Bartender's Book**
Everything **Bedtime Story Book**
Everything **Beer Book**
Everything **Bicycle Book**
Everything **Bird Book**
Everything **Build Your Own Home Page Book**
Everything **Casino Gambling Book**
Everything **Cat Book**
Everything® **Christmas Book**
Everything **College Survival Book**
Everything **Cover Letter Book**
Everything **Crossword and Puzzle Book**
Everything **Dating Book**
Everything **Dessert Book**
Everything **Dog Book**
Everything **Dreams Book**
Everything **Etiquette Book**
Everything **Family Tree Book**

Everything **Fly-Fishing Book**
Everything **Games Book**
Everything **Get-a-Job Book**
Everything **Get Published Book**
Everything **Get Ready For Baby Book**
Everything **Golf Book**
Everything **Guide to New York City**
Everything **Guide to Walt Disney World®, Universal Studios®, and Greater Orlando**
Everything **Guide to Washington D.C.**
Everything **Herbal Remedies Book**
Everything **Homeselling Book**
Everything **Homebuying Book**
Everything **Home Improvement Book**
Everything **Internet Book**
Everything **Investing Book**
Everything **Jewish Wedding Book**
Everything **Kids' Money Book**
Everything **Kids' Nature Book**
Everything **Kids' Puzzle Book**
Everything **Low-Fat High-Flavor Cookbook**
Everything **Microsoft® Word 2000 Book**

Everything **Money Book**
Everything **One-Pot Cookbook**
Everything **Online Business Book**
Everything **Online Investing Book**
Everything **Pasta Book**
Everything **Pregnancy Book**
Everything **Pregnancy Organizer**
Everything **Resume Book**
Everything **Sailing Book**
Everything **Selling Book**
Everything **Study Book**
Everything **Tarot Book**
Everything **Toasts Book**
Everything **Total Fitness Book**
Everything **Trivia Book**
Everything **Tropical Fish Book**
Everything® **Wedding Book, 2nd Edition**
Everything® **Wedding Checklist**
Everything® **Wedding Etiquette Book**
Everything® **Wedding Organizer**
Everything® **Wedding Shower Book**
Everything® **Wedding Vows Book**
Everything **Wine Book**